CW00539042

A DECADE OF PROGRESS

VIRGIN TRAINS
A DECADE OF PROGRESS

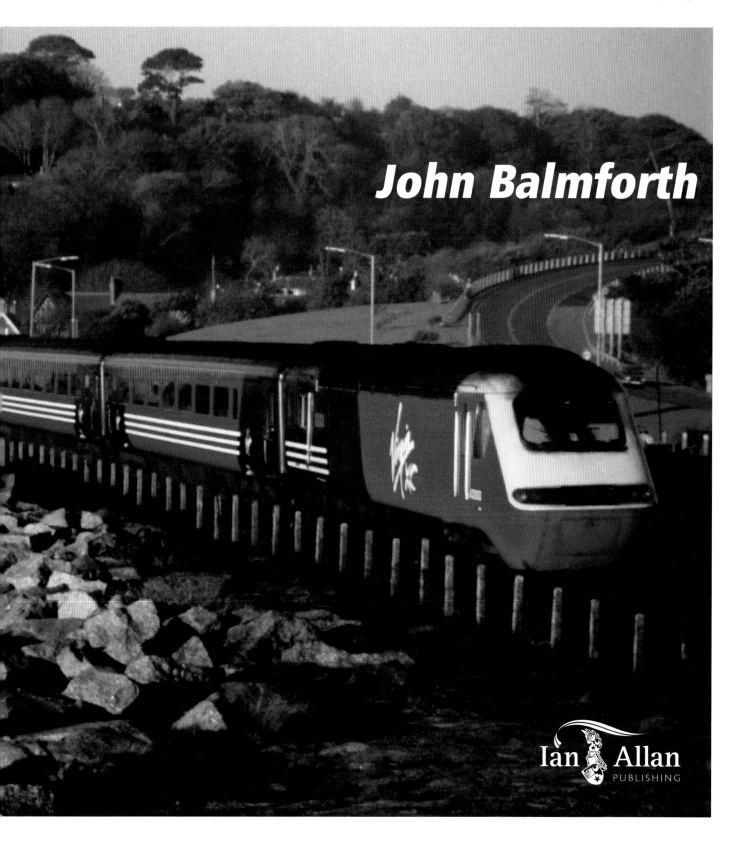

John Balmforth

Ian Allan
PUBLISHING

Contents

First published 2007

ISBN (10) 0 7110 3224 6
ISBN (13) 978 0 7110 3224 8

Published by Ian Allan Publishing

an imprint of Ian Allan Publishing Ltd, Hersham, Surrey KT12 4RG.
Printed in England by Ian Allan Printing Ltd, Hersham, Surrey KT12 4RG.

Code: 0704/A3

Visit the Ian Allan Publishing website at
www.ianallanpublishing.com

Front cover: **West Coast Pendolino and CrossCountry Super Voyager rest between turns at Manchester Piccadilly in August 2002.** *Virgin Trains / Milepost 92¹ᐟ²*

Back cover, top. **Seen on a damp winters night at Preston is a Class 57/3 Virgin Thunderbird coming to the rescue of a stricken Class 87 which had failed whilst hauling a Pendolino on test in 2004.** *Virgin Trains / Milepost 92¹ᐟ²*

Back cover bottom: **Approaching Bristol Temple Meads in a Voyager as another train passes, heading north, on 5 November 2005.** *John Balmforth*

Half-title page: **A CrossCountry Voyager leaves the down main line near Chesterfield station to take the Down Barrow Hill line, known locally as the 'Old Road'.** *Virgin Trains / Milepost 92¹ᐟ²*

Title page: **The 'Cornishman' nears Penzance at the end of its day-long CrossCountry service from Aberdeen.** *Virgin Trains / Milepost 92¹ᐟ²*

Right: **A rare sight indeed as a 16-car Virgin Voyager four-set train crosses the Royal Border Bridge at Berwick upon Tweed in 2002 while on a test run. This is the maximum length at which Voyagers are authorised to operate.** *Virgin Trains / Milepost 92¹ᐟ²*

RAILWAY children

THE VOICE FOR STREET CHILDREN WORLDWIDE

The Railway Children charity
Registered Charity No 1058991

The Railway Children charity helps runaway and abandoned children who live in and around the world's railway stations. Working through partner organisations, the charity offers shelter, healthcare, education, training, protection and, above all, friendship.

The work of The Railway Children would not be possible without the generosity of its supporters. There are many ways you can help the charity help the millions of street children around the world. Thanks to loyal supporters, The Railway Children now helps around 7,000 children every year, and also makes contact with and counsel or refer on about another 12,000.

All of the royalties due to the author from the sale of this book are being donated to The Railway Children charity.

You can read more about the charity on its web site at http:/www.railwaychildren.org.uk and should you wish to support the charity, donations can be sent to:

The Railway Children
Unit G 14,
Scope House,
Weston Road,
Crewe,
Cheshire
CW1 6DD
United Kingdom

Foreword

t is a little-known fact, but the first ever idea for Virgin to get involved in the rail industry actually came from British Rail itself!

Dr John Prideaux had been talking to Chris Moss, the then marketing director of Virgin Atlantic, about the possibility of the airline having its own carriage on the Gatwick Express.

Chris happened to discuss the idea with me while I was on a Japanese bullet train with Will Whitehorn in early 1991, and my thoughts and conversation that day turned rapidly from why to WHY NOT? Roll forward a year and the caste that would shape the future of Britain's high-speed railways began to emerge.

The Tory government wanted to privatise the railways and we were frustrated with the shortage of take-off slots at Heathrow to allow us to really compete with BA. The idea of creating the kind of speed, frequency and quality of trains necessary to attract people back to rail on busy air routes like Manchester–London became a passion.

During this time I first met people like Chris Green, Jim Steer, Rupert Darwell, Patrick McCall, Richard Bowker, Robin Gisby and Tony Collins, some of whom feature in the story. One thing they all shared was a vision of a new railway taking advantage of tilting train technology finally able to give long-suffering customers the quiet, comfortable and fast services they deserved.

It was in January 1997 that Virgin Trains was born. From the start we knew we had a challenge and wisely couched our promises in the reality of the timescale we knew it would take to fulfil them, but even we did not realise the full horror of the state of the infrastructure, or the storm that was about to unfold as our rail industry tore itself apart in the wake of tragic accidents, and the collapse of Railtrack.

But promises are promises and I supported the Virgin team in the red corner battling their way through every misfortune the four horsemen of the apocalypse could throw at them. It is a fascinating tale well described in this warts-and-all account of the biggest infrastructure project Britain has seen since the Second World War. So often they had to fight the cynics in their own industry who had insisted we would never get the trains to work and that our plans were 'up in the clouds'.

As it turned out, those cynics were wrong and we now have a long-distance railway to be proud of. It has captured more than half the airline market between Manchester and London, created some world firsts on the way, and proved the old 19th century business concept of 'build it and they will come' can still be true today.

I cannot take the credit for that, but rather would like to take this opportunity to thank the thousands of Virgin employees who kept the faith in the worst of times and held onto the belief that we could deliver if given the chance.

We have also had great support from those in Network Rail and government who picked up the phoenix out of the ashes and carried on through to allow the Pendolino and Voyagers to do what they do best.

Next stop 135mph.

Sir Richard Branson,
Chairman Virgin Group.
Virgin Trains / Milepost 92¹ᐟ²

Sir Richard Branson
March 2007

Introduction

I left the rail industry in 1996 when it was finally broken into small pieces for privatisation, believing there could be no job left to match running the national InterCity network. I was wrong, because when Richard Branson rang me two years later to invite me to run his new Virgin Trains company, I immediately realised both the awesome scale of the challenge ahead – and the fun of working for such a highly supportive entrepreneur.

Virgin Trains had won the core of InterCity with two exceptionally creative bids for CrossCountry and West Coast. Between them, they accounted for 40 per cent of all InterCity travel in the United Kingdom (UK) and provide the only remaining national network stretching from Aberdeen to Penzance.

Virgin Trains had also succeeded in delivering the investment that InterCity had been denied for a decade. The West Coast Main Line was to be totally upgraded at last. The entire CrossCountry and West Coast train fleets were to be renewed (InterCity had never even dared to think of new trains for CrossCountry) – and tilting trains would return to the UK after the failure of the Advanced Passenger Train.

These are still two of the most imaginative and daring franchise bids yet made, and were only surpassed by Virgin Trains' cheeky bid a few years later on for the East Coast – complete with a brand-new 185mph high-speed line.

I joined Virgin Trains in 1999 to lead the two train companies through the most daunting transitional period that any train company has faced. All our Christmases had arrived in terms of investment, but I knew that we faced a living hell when contractors started working on a live railway carrying 15 million passengers a year. Wrong again. It proved to be twice as hellish as even I had expected. We only survived by inspiring a wartime spirit in a brilliant team of staff – old and new.

John Balmforth lived through this experience in his parallel universe in the Rail Passengers Committee for the Midlands. He was at the sharp end of numerous customer, media and local government complaints and he was at the interface with Virgin Trains, Railtrack and & Network Rail managers, encouraging them as they struggled to give birth to their £8 billion baby. John demonstrates a real feel for the rail industry, and it is typical of the man that he is donating all of his royalties from the sale of this book to the Railway Children charity.

Chris Green, Virgin Trains' Chief Executive 1999–2004, subsequently Virgin Rail Group Chairman.
Virgin Trains / Milepost 92$^{1/2}$

His book captures the epic struggle in an even-handed and observant style. He opens with the exhilaration of finally getting the investment to modernise the West Coast Main Line and leads on to the early disappointments in customer service; the disbelief over the Hatfield speed restrictions and the frustrations of trying to operate a railway that became the biggest building site in Europe.

Above all, he captures the amazing resilience, humour and sheer professionalism of a team of 3,000 Virgin Trains staff who had to face their customers every day knowing that the next crisis was probably not far away. This is their story, and it deserves to be told.

Chris Green
Chief Executive Virgin Trains (1999–2004)
March 2007

Privatisation: *a brief outline*

John Major's Conservative government was successful in the 1992 General Election with a mandate that the railways would pass into private ownership. The government's manifesto did not indicate what form this should be in, neither did it indicate how the network should be divided up. It is thought that the British Railways Board favoured the business being sold as a going concern, in similar fashion to many of the utility companies. However, that model was not chosen and one which favoured the railway infrastructure being separated from the actual provision of passenger and freight services was adopted. A new company, Railtrack, was formed to take over the ownership and management of the infrastructure. Unlike the Train Operating Companies (TOCs) whose tenure required the winning of a franchise, Railtrack was a licensed custodian, effectively owning its assets in perpetuity, provided it did not breach its licence seriously, but its relatively early demise was, as we shall see later in the book, to have a serious effect on Virgin's West Coast franchise in particular.

While some blamed nationalisation for the failure to modernise the West Coast Main Line, it was really down to the attitude of the Treasury, which deliberately delayed things pre-1992 and then delayed privatisation for a further six years. So, for privatisation to be politically accepted this needed to be achieved through the franchising process. The Office of Passenger Rail Franchising (OPRAF) was responsible for letting the new franchises and in a bid to obtain an acceptable outcome agreed a core investment programme with Railtrack. This required the route to be enhanced to modern standards and included a package to upgrade the track and power supplies to 125mph standards using tilting trains. The Virgin West Coast bid took matters one step further with plans for 140mph running using new state-of-the-art Pendolino (Italian for tilting) trains.

The passenger operations of British Rail were divided into 25 franchises. The holders of the franchises were required to enter into a track access agreement with Railtrack allowing them to use the infrastructure. At the time of privatisation the InterCity sector was operating 'in the black', but the new access charges were set to approximately double the equivalent operating costs of British Rail days. The idea was that the additional income would go towards bringing the infrastructure back to good order. The adding of leasing fees for rolling stock being paid to the rolling stock companies (ROSCOs) meant that TOCs would require subsidy payments from OPRAF. It was rather ironic that the total required to compensate train operators for the higher access charges was £1.6 million in 1994/95, an increase of almost 58 per cent on the previous year, British Rail's last. Staffing, training and station costs added further to operator liabilities and with fares being the only real source of income, it was clear that government support would be required for some franchises well into their franchise period, although ultimately it was intended that most operators would be paying a premium before their franchise ended.

The CrossCountry and West Coast franchises were amongst the more difficult and complex, in particular that of the West Coast where the infrastructure was in a very poor state. Partly because of this they were amongst the last franchises to be let, with the West Coast bid including major upgrade proposals.

One of Virgin CrossCountry's HSTs encounters high seas on the Dawlish sea wall in 2001 as it heads for Penzance.
Virgin Trains / Milepost 92$^{1/2}$

Why railways?

During the early days of my research for this book I kept coming back to the same question – 'Why did Virgin and Richard Branson want to become involved with railways?' Why would he risk the good reputation of the Virgin brand by becoming involved in an industry that so often appeared to let itself down?

Back in the mid-1990s, Britain's rail network had been ridiculed in many quarters for years and was targeted by many a comedian. Indeed, there can be no disputing that the network was generally in a very run-down condition with considerable areas of infrastructure in need of modernisation, and rolling stock that was, in the public's eye, already well past its 'sell by date'.

Probably the most successful part of the Virgin empire at that time was the airline, Virgin Atlantic. It had built itself a solid reputation for service provision and, for many, it was the preferred choice of carrier and Sir Richard Branson's name is inexorably linked with Virgin. Although there were doubters, many people loved and trusted both names, so why was Sir Richard prepared to risk these hard-won reputations? Part of the answer was eventually supplied by Will Whitehorn of the Virgin Management Group.

Virgin Atlantic operates long-haul air services from London's Heathrow and Gatwick airports and eyeing seamless travel, Virgin recognised the need to get its passengers, many of whom were based in the north of England or Scotland, to and from the airport quickly and efficiently. It seemed logical to attempt to do this by providing efficient high-speed train services but unfortunately a plan to run a high-speed service each way daily between the north and the Capital did not come to fruition. It followed that when the government announced its intention to privatise the railways that Virgin would have an interest in bidding for the West Coast rail franchise. However, Virgin Atlantic's customers needed to travel to all parts of the UK and the CrossCountry franchise would also provide this link from the south west areas of the country.

A Class 87 electric locomotive pauses at Birmingham New Street on 23 April 2005, having just arrived with a train from London Euston. *Michael Hughes*

Virgin Trains Class 87
No 87010 *King Arthur*
awaits departure from
London Euston with the
09.10 service to
Birmingham New Street
on 5 May 2005.
Stuart Baker

Virgin Trains Chief Executive (2006) Tony Collins also explained that Virgin was prepared to take business risks, attempting projects others were not prepared to get involved with. Moving into the railways reflects this, but Sir Richard Branson would not have done so if he had not felt that Virgin could make a difference to the industry.

The Virgin entrepreneur was well aware of the successes attributed to high-speed rail services elsewhere in the world and realised that it ought to be possible to replicate this within the United Kingdom, although it would need considerable investment. The West Coast Main Line was in desperate need of such investment, but the responsibility for that had passed to Railtrack for the infrastructure, and the ROSCOs for the trains themselves following the privatisation of Britain's railways. If Virgin wished to emulate the growing success of its airline on the railways it would be necessary to enter a partnership with these players, but first the franchises had to be secured.

The two franchises were bid for and on 29 November 1996 it was announced that the CrossCountry franchise was being awarded to Virgin Rail Group for a 15-year 3-month period commencing on 5 January 1997. The West Coast franchise was also awarded to the Virgin Rail Group on 19 February 1997 and signed shortly afterwards on 9 March 1997, for 15 years. The now-famous red trains with white 'go-faster' stripes, affectionately known as 'Kit Kat livery' would soon become familiar to rail passengers throughout Britain. Sir Richard Branson made a famous promise that he would replace all of the old trains with brand-new ones, thus providing Virgin's rail passengers with trains fit for the 21st century.

Passengers used to the high quality service associated with the Virgin brand expected to see massive changes overnight, encouraged by the immediate appearance of the Virgin logo on the trains themselves. With hindsight this was possibly a mistake because it was never going to be possible and in a very short time rumblings of discontent began to surface and the realisation that improvements would take time led to con-siderable negative comment, by passengers, the press and the media. Sir Richard's promise was kept though, and this is the story of the roller coaster ride that saw complete replacement of the fleet by 2004 using state-of-the-art Voyager (Class 220), Super Voyager (Class 221) and Pendolino (Class 390) trains. The latter are capable of 140mph and Classes 221 and 390 are able to tilt to maintain high average speeds and achieve enhanced timings.

Although they are distinct independent com-panies, both CrossCountry Trains Limited and West Coast Trains Limited are often referred to by the combined brand name of 'Virgin Trains'.

Both companies are component parts of the controlling Virgin Rail Group which is owned 51 per cent by Virgin Management (part of the Virgin Group headed by Sir Richard Branson) and 49 per cent by Stagecoach. The latter had been founded in 1980 by brother and sister team Brian Souter and Ann Gloag, operating two buses in Perth, Scotland. The company is still based there today even though it has grown into a major interna-tional transport organisation, and its vehicles are a common sight on roads across the UK.

Stagecoach's first venture into the UK rail network came in the summer of 1992 when it pro-vided two standard class carriages, painted in the company livery, in the overnight Aberdeen-London passenger train. Despite providing road feeder services the rail business struggled, though it did not deter Stagecoach from future involvement in railways. In December 2005 the government announced that Stagecoach had won the bidding for the South West Trains franchise. August 1996 saw the company make a successful bid to purchase one of Britain's leading rolling stock leasing companies, Porterbrook Leasing, at the same time giving assurances that it would not offer preferential prices to its own rail subsidiaries.

Stagecoach had previously shown an interest in the West Coast and CrossCountry franchises before they were won by Virgin Rail. Virgin Group initially owned 42% of the franchises with the balance being held by four venture capitalists, who wanted Virgin Rail floated on the stock market. However, Sir Richard Branson and Brian Souter entered negotiations and brokered an alternative deal which saw Virgin Group's holding increased to 51% whilst Stagecoach purchased 49% for £108million cash plus £50million in Stagecoach shares.

Until recently, the Chairman of Virgin Rail Group was the highly respected Chris Green, who has now moved on to membership of the board of Network Rail. He had previously been the Chief Executive of Virgin Trains and successfully overseen the introduction to service of the new train fleet. Patrick McCall replaced him at the helm.

His successor as Chief Executive at Virgin Trains is Tony Collins who was promoted from within the company. The Managing Directors at CrossCountry Trains Limited and West Coast Trains Limited are Chris Gibb and Charles Belcher respectively. Their professional capability, as that of Chris Green, is widely respected within the rail industry. They have both been managing directors at other train operating companies before joining Virgin Trains.

It is an inescapable fact that the privatisation of British Rail resulted in the rail industry losing several high-quality career railwaymen. Some of them, like Chris Green, eventually returned and it is sometimes mentioned that Railtrack did not have enough 'railwaymen' at the top. Without doubt, all train operating companies do need the expertise of such professionals, but it should not be forgotten that the private sector supplied highly capable businessmen who brought with them many years of experience in commercial and contracts issues. They had the necessary skills to create visionary contracts to take the railway forward. One such person is Virgin Trains' Tony Collins. He told the author: 'The contracts Virgin set in place with train builders and Railtrack were visionary, and were strictly enforced. Without the tight contracts we would not have seen the delivery of the new train fleets'. He may, of course, be correct and the blend of private sector and government has been a crucial factor in taking Virgin Trains (VT) forward. It can be seen that VT has the mix of experienced railwaymen and private sector commercial experience at its helm. This can only be of immense value as Virgin develops its rail franchises.

Both franchises would subsequently undergo financial difficulties, (the reasons are covered later in this book), and operated services under letters of agreement with the SRA. These were effectively a supplement to the existing franchise contracts. Whilst there are differences of opinion as to whether the original contracts were parked or even suspended it is a fact that the track access agreement under PUG 2 is still the basis giving Virgin Trains the right to operate trains along the route of the originally planned upgraded output.

In heritage blue livery, No 87001 *Stephenson* departs from Crewe at the rear of its soon-to-be-withdrawn rake of Mk 3 coaches and a DVT, in 2005. *Peter W. Robinson*

The West Coast Main Line:
a brief description

The principal services on the West Coast Main Line link London with major cities at Birmingham, Wolverhampton, Crewe, Manchester, Preston, Carlisle and Glasgow. A number of other important places are also served and the route also sees services to Holyhead (for boat train connections to Ireland).

The name West Coast Main Line (WCML) can be little misleading since a passenger travelling its entire length will only ever get a brief glimpse of the sea, just north of Lancaster. More accurately it runs up the western side of England and Scotland. However there are two direct rail routes from London to Scotland and since one runs up the eastern side of the country and the other up the west it was an easy way to differentiate routes to be taken by particular trains. Hence we have the East Coast Main Line and the West Coast Main Line.

The WCML, as with the CrossCountry route, was not built as a complete entity, but is the result of the gradual merging of a number of railway companies and routes over a period of around 40 years. Component parts first came together as the London & North Western Railway (LNWR) in England, and the Caledonian Railway in Scotland, the two later forming a major part of the London Midland & Scottish Railway (LMS) in 1923. Later, this company was nationalised, becoming a part of British Railways on 1 January 1948.

The first train from London Euston over part of the route operated in 1838 and ran as far as Birmingham. Completion of the route through to Glasgow and Edinburgh was achieved in February 1848. After consolidation of the early English railway companies into the London & North Western Railway, a process not completed until 1859, the route soon came to be considered and promoted as the 'Premier Line'. Nearly a century later, in 1955, proposals were made under British Railway's Modernisation Plan for the line to be electrified from London to Liverpool and Manchester, including the loop via Birmingham and Wolverhampton. To call a line a 'loop' when it serves major cities such as Coventry, Birmingham and Wolverhampton seems odd to the layman, but it is terminology still used today even with the additional calling point added at Birmingham International – a major airport serving destinations all over the world.

These proposals began to reach fruition when the southern section of the line was modernised between 1959 and 1966. This upgrading effectively saw the end of the regular use of steam-

Another Class 87 departs Coventry in 2003 at the rear of a 'push-pull' train for London Euston.
Virgin Trains / Milepost 92$^{1/2}$

hauled trains on this part of the West Coast Main Line, bringing with it new electric locomotives, rolling stock and stations. The upgrade was a huge success with the first year seeing the railway attracting an increase of some 70 per cent in passenger numbers. The rest of the route was upgraded in the early 1970s with the new electric services between London and Glasgow commencing in May 1974.

No further modernisation in real terms was made to the route for almost three decades, not until after the 15-year franchise to operate passenger services was awarded to Virgin West Coast in 1997.

The lack of earlier funding resulted in the new franchise holder initially having to run elderly trains, some approaching their 30th year, over a worn-out infrastructure. However, Virgin Trains successful bid for the franchise included a commitment to replace the entire fleet and this, coupled with an agreement from Railtrack that the WCML would be completely upgraded with line speeds enhanced to 140mph, meant that the train operator was confident that it would be able to eliminate the need for government subsidy approximately half way through its franchise.

Unfortunately, the upgrade costs were spiralling ever upwards and the original estimated cost of £2 billion proved impossible to achieve. Railtrack's demise saw its successor, Network Rail, take over the upgrade and at one point the estimated final cost had risen dramatically to almost £13 billion. By 2000, Railtrack had announced that the 140mph top speed would not be achieved and the route would only be upgraded to 125mph running. Subsequent fur-

ther cost savings reduced the estimated final bill to £7.8 billion. Even so, a brand-new fleet of 53 tilting electric Pendolino trains has entered service with the addition of two of the Super Voyager diesel trains for use on the non-electrified section of route to Holyhead. In addition, West Coast Trains Ltd has 16 Class 57/3 'Thunderbird' locomotives which can be used as rescue locomotives or to drag Pendolinos on diversions over non-electrified routes. These are also used to rescue any other operators failed trains in order to keep the routes open to traffic, and feature a 2,750hp engine enabling a top speed of 95mph.

The West Coast franchise has seen a dramatic increase in the number of passengers being carried which has resulted in each of the Pendolino trains receiving an additional ninth coach.

Above: **A busy scene at Coventry in 2002 as a West Coast train for London Euston passes a northbound CrossCountry service, while a local Central Trains Class 323 EMU waits at platform 4.** *Virgin Trains / Milepost 92$^{1/2}$*

Below: **The final rake of Mk 2 coaches in service with West Coast is headed into Oxley depot by a Class 87 locomotive bearing a commemorative headboard, on 15 June 2004.** *Virgin Trains / Milepost 92$^{1/2}$*

Virgin West Coast
(West Coast Trains Ltd)

Virgin Trains took control of the West Coast franchise on 9 March 1997 and unlike CrossCountry, most of its services were operated by electric traction. Class 86 and 87 locomotives hauled Mk 2 or Mk 3 carriages, although a number of services used High Speed Train diesels. However, the rolling stock was pretty well life expired and the infrastructure too was well past its 'sell by date'. Massive investment would be needed if the Virgin Trains vision of a world-class railway was to be achieved. For the West Coast fleet this would require an investment of £590 million by Angel Trains (one of the Rolling Stock Leasing Companies) with a further £500 million in whole-life maintenance. On top of that would be the ultimate £8 billion to finance the West Coast Route Modernisation. Virgin Trains itself would eventually need to be paying premiums totalling £1.6 billion to OPRAF.

The fleet of locomotives inherited by Virgin Trains with the West Coast franchise were:

Class	Type	Number	Built
08	diesel shunter	9	1955 to 1962
43	HST	6	1982
86	electric	7	1965 to 1966
87	electric	35	1973 to 1974
90	electric	15	1987 to 1990

In addition, West Coast inherited a number of sets of Mk 2 carriages built 1973-75 and Mk 3s built 1977-85. These were used in push-pull mode using driving van trailers (DVT) on the opposite end of the train to the locomotive.

Towards the end of the last century, Chris Green, then Virgin Trains Chief Executive, gave the George Curry Memorial lecture to the Institute of Mechanical Engineers. He entitled the lecture 'West Coast the Third Dawn'. He describes the 'first false dawn' as being the 1980s. This was the era of the Advanced Passenger Train (APT) and the plan was to have some 60 of these trains in service by the middle of the decade. The first demonstration run set the UK speed record at 160mph in December 1979. Five years on, the journey time from London to Glasgow was slashed to 3 hours 53 minutes on 12 December 1984. So why a false dawn? Well, because the achievements were not taken the next step further, following reversals of a technical nature, an issue which did not deter engineers – nor the financing governments – in Italy or Sweden.

The 'second false dawn' he saw as the 1990s, Chris Green holding the view that a booming economy and the entrepreneurial attitudes unleashed by Sir Robert Reid's reorganisation of the railway allowed InterCity to take another look at the West Coast Main Line. Although a tilting train was not being envisaged a plan for a new 155mph conventional train emerged. It was to be called InterCity 250 (IC 250) and would have seen a London–Manchester journey time of just two hours. Considerable effort and detail was put into the project and a full-scale mock-up was created of both cab and passenger interiors. So why another false dawn? This time the economy crashed in the early 1990s and the IC 250 project was cancelled in July 1992. It was a real pity because, in fact, the East Coast Main Line had recently undergone successful modernisation.

In the aftermath of the cancellation of IC 250 an influential lobby group West Coast Rail 250 (WCR 250), was formed. This was done on the initiative of Carlisle City and Cumbria County Councils, with the strong support of Eric Martlew, MP for Carlisle, who also led the All-Party Parliamentary Group on the West Coast Main Line. WCR 250 had soon won support from more than 80 local authorities throughout the West Coast network, and working closely with the All-Party Group, started a serious lobbying campaign for the re-instatement of investment in the route. In 1993, it commissioned

Waiting at Birmingham International to make its final journey for Virgin West Coast on 15 June 2004 is a rake of Mk 2 carriages. Invited guests travelled on the train to Wolverhampton and on to Oxley where the carriages were taken out of service.
Virgin Trains

Steer Davies Gleeve to undertake a study into the costs and benefits of developing the West Coast Main Line as a high speed route – with very positive results. These were presented at a major conference in Manchester Town Hall in the summer of 1994 attended by delegates from all parts of the system, potential bidders for the franchise, and the Minister of State for Railways. Copies of the reports were also deposited at the Office for Passenger Rail Franchising with their collections of documents for bidders for the West Coast franchise.

When the Chancellor of the Exchequer, the Rt Hon. Kenneth Clarke MP, announced in his budget statement in 1993 that £150 million would be made available for investment in new rolling stock for British Rail, WCR 250 worked closely with Inter-City West Coast to try to secure that for the route. This would have seen a new-build of 12 to 15 InterCity 225 trains similar to those which had recently been built for the East Coast Main Line. The campaign included a demonstration run from Glasgow Central to London Euston, meetings with ministers and the Chairman of the British Railways Board, but eventually the funding went to the supply of new trains for Network SouthEast.

The 'third dawn' was not a false one, Chris Green enthused. This was the era which saw the privatisation of the railways and one which re-ignited the desire to see an upgrade to the West Coast Main Line. It was also an era which saw Virgin Trains win the West Coast franchise.

Virgin Rail Group had entered into a partnership with Railtrack and the Rolling Stock Leasing Companies which would, ultimately, result in fast tilting trains running in service on the West Coast Main Line. An issue now would be signalling. Certainly 140mph could not be achieved using like-for-like replacement signalling equipment.

Consultants' recommended that moving block signalling would be the best way of providing a low-risk low-cost solution. This would require on-train equipment providing real-time data on train speed and position to a central processor by digital radio. The central processor would then radio back a maximum speed and limit of movement authority to the train, with this information being displayed in the cab.

At the same time, Europe's railways and signalling industry had been working on the European Train Control System (ETCS). This is an expandable system with three levels:

Level 1 – puts balises down on the track connected to the existing lineside signalling equipment giving Automatic Train Protection (ATP).

The penultimate Euston–Carlisle service to be worked by a locomotive and Mk 3 coaches curves through Leyland near Preston in September 2004.
Virgin Trains / Milepost 92½

A Class 87 locomotive heading a set of Mk 3s and a DVT pauses at Birmingham International with a northbound service in 2003.
Virgin Trains / Milepost 92½

Above: **A West Coast Class 90 electric locomotive on a service for London Euston departs Crewe in 2003, at the rear of a rake of Mk 3 carriages and a DVT.**
Virgin Trains / Milepost 92$^{1/2}$

Right: **One of West Coast's newly repainted Class 90s, No 90011 rests between turns at London Euston.**
Virgin Trains / Milepost 92$^{1/2}$

Below: **Two Virgin West Coast driving van trailers (DVTs) stand side-by-side at journeys' end after heading their trains into London Euston in 2004.**
Peter W. Robinson

Level 2 – also uses the existing lineside signalling equipment and track circuits to detect trains but it adds cab signalling. This requires the installation of a computer which analyses traditional signalling and then sends a message to the cab of a high speed train to provide advance notice of signal settings ahead of the train. These are updated every few seconds and read up to six balises ahead thus instructing the train on its maximum speed profile and movement authority.

Level 3 – is the full version which also gets rid of track circuits and other fixed lineside equipment, together with their associated maintenance costs.

Railtrack had intimated that it intended to go for the full Level 3 version which does not require

Left: **A West Coast DVT at the head of a London bound service passes a CrossCountry Voyager as it thunders through Stafford.** *Virgin Trains / Milepost 92¹/²*

Below: **A West Coast London-bound service speeds south along the West Coast Main Line near Tamworth in 2004.** *Virgin Trains / Milepost 92¹/²*

Bottom: **One of the last locomotive plus Mk 3s to work south, on a Glasgow Central–Euston service passes milepost 145 south of Crewe with the loco propelling, in 2004.** *Virgin Trains / Milepost 92¹/²*

track circuits and other fixed lineside equipment. However, whilst Virgin Trains' plan for West Coast would be satisfactorily controlled by conventional signalling until 2002, it would require the more advanced version to accommodate the planned 140mph operation in 2005. Realising the time pressure it faced Railtrack scaled down to Level 2. This would meet Virgin Trains immediate requirements and could be upgraded a step further at a later date if required, but to meet their business plan West Coast would need to have the trains, in Chris Green's words, 'running comfortably full'.

Whilst this system would be ideal it was not yet reliable enough to be included operationally in the upgrade, and the new trains entered service using the present-day multiple aspect colour light signalling. Whilst this can still sustain high speed running braking distances would be critical and the author feels that until more reliable advanced signalling technology is in place the goal of 140mph will continue to remain difficult to attain. It is really rather sad that although the rail industry in the UK has been able to supply the innovative train design to achieve high speeds, the full benefits remain out of reach because of the seeming inability to provide a matching infrastructure at the right price. The opportunity may well be lost forever; effectively another false dawn.

The initial estimated cost of the required infrastructure upgrade was £2.1 billion, and as stated earlier, this subsequently rose alarmingly to almost an unbelievable estimate of £13 billion before being reduced to £7.8 billion, a much more acceptable level of overall cost. Despite the cut in costs and the earlier reduction in line speed to 125mph very significant journey time reductions were still achieved resulting in Virgin West Coast posing a serious competitive threat to even the cut price airlines serving the major cities on

Above right: **A Virgin West Coast service heads south along the West Coast Main Line near Great Strickland, Cumbria during 2002.**
Virgin Trains / Milepost 92$^{1/2}$

Right: **Let the train take the strain. A Virgin West Coast express heads for London alongside the M1 at Watford Gap in 2001.**
Virgin Trains / Milepost 92$^{1/2}$

Below: **Virgin Trains DVT No 82126 stands at Manchester Piccadilly waiting to depart with a service to London Euston.**
Virgin Trains / Milepost 92$^{1/2}$

the British mainland. The reduction in line-speed was to pose a major obstacle to Virgin Trains ability to achieve its aim of additional service trains running with considerable reductions in journey times, but West Coast still attracted significant increases in the numbers of passengers being carried.

Earlier, Railtrack had committed itself to upgrading the West Coast Main Line by replacing like with like and raising speed limits to 125mph on parts of the route. This became known as Passenger Upgrade 1 (PUG 1), later to be renamed West Coast Route Modernisation Phase 1. Virgin Trains was not impressed with reaching 125mph, after all this was not really any improvement on what had been achieved in 1979 by HSTs on other major routes in Britain. Instead, Virgin Trains was convinced that

Above: **Its paintwork reflecting in the adjacent canal, a West Coast service heads along the Trent Valley route north of Rugby.**
Virgin Trains / Milepost 92$^{1/2}$

Left: **Three different modes of transport are seen in this view as a West Coast service departs Glasgow Central for London Euston in 2002.**
Virgin Trains / Milepost 92$^{1/2}$

Below left: **Loco-hauled trains on southbound and northbound West Coast expresses pass near Crewe.**
Virgin Trains / Milepost 92$^{1/2}$

Above: **A West Coast HST takes a well-earned rest at Holyhead after arriving with a well-filled service from London Euston on 15 May 2005.** *Peter W. Robinson*

Above left: **A Virgin West Coast train at Proof House Junction leaves Birmingham New Street with a service for London Euston in 2001.**
Virgin Trains / Milepost 92¹ᐟ²

Left:**A West Coast DVT heads a push-pull Mk 3 set across the Mersey Bridge at Runcorn, on a Liverpool Lime Street–London Euston service.**
Virgin Trains / Milepost 92¹ᐟ²

Below: **A Virgin West Coast High Speed Train (HST) departs Bangor with a service for Holyhead in 2003.**
Virgin Trains / Milepost 92¹ᐟ²

140mph running could be attained. VT's own plans required the upgrade to be taken a step further to allow its new tilting trains to run at their 140mph design speed, a significant improvement on its basic West Coast franchise requirement. The company considered this to be essential if it were to fulfil Sir Richard Branson's promise of a world-class railway fit for the 21st century. Commercially, it would be vital that the end to end speed of the line could compete with other modes of transport. Virgin West Coast had a vision to increase the number of inter-city trains leaving London's Euston station to the north from five per hour in 1997 to an incredible eleven trains per hour each way by 2005. With trains running more or less every five minutes the aim was to get motorists out of cars and onto the trains, and also show airline passengers that rail was a viable alternative means of travel.

Although ambitious, Virgin Trains franchise bid for the West Coast was based upon 140mph running. To help achieve this Virgin announced that it was entering into an agreement with Railtrack whereby 80 per cent of Railtrack's expected £600 million investment would be underwritten by Virgin West Coast's additional track access charges that would fall due with the higher speeds. The remainder would come from a unique revenue-sharing deal between the two companies, but it would only work if Railtrack delivered on journey time, capacity and reliability. If all were delivered on time, both companies would prosper, but tilting trains were also a key part of the plan. Without them the higher speed would not be consistently attainable over set distances. Despite the required increase in speed this in itself was not the biggest challenge – that was to be capacity. It naturally followed that this

further enhancement would become Passenger Upgrade 2 (PUG 2) subsequently renamed West Coast Route Modernisation Phase 2. The penalties for failing to deliver on time would, to quote Chris Green, have 'dwarfed anything seen or threatened to date'.

The agreement itself included provision for 140mph to be reached a mere five miles out of Euston and to be able to be maintained for 85 per cent of the way to Crewe. Railtrack also had to agree to provide capacity for other users of the West Coast Main Line. This included providing 42 extra freight paths per day by 2005 without degrading other services, something which Railtrack struggled with almost from the start of the agreement.

The PUG 2 agreement guaranteed access for eleven Pendolinos per hour out of Euston from 06.00–22.00, 363 days per year without engineering perturbation, but even on a brand-new railway this would surely have been impossible to achieve. When the announcement was made by Railtrack in 2002 that PUG 2 would be descoped it became known as 'Black Diamond Day' in the industry.

The West Coast Main Line upgrade

In June 2003 The Strategic Rail Authority published it's Strategy for the West Coast Main Line aimed at formulating clear strategies for build of the route that specified the best use of the network balancing service provision, maintenance access and performance levels. The Authority's 2003 strategy programme included:-

- Addressing a major backlog in maintenance and renewals; achieving value for money.

- Establishing sustainable maintenance regimes.

Engineers at work in 2004 replacing a junction on the southern section of the West Coast Main Line.
railphotolibrary.com

The upgrade of the West Coast Main Line included the complete replacement of Proof House Junction, just outside Birmingham New Street station.
railphotolibrary.com

■ Providing capacity for anticipated growth in passenger (80 per cent more long distance trains) and freight business (60-70 per cent more capacity) over the next 20-30 years.

■ Securing an improved level of performance (90 per cent of long distance trains arriving within 10 minutes of the advertised time), safety and reliability, helping the railway to regain lost market share and increase the role it plays in the national and regional economies.

■ Achieve these on a working railway.

By the time the West Coast Main Line Upgrade progress report was published in May 2006, the role of the SRA had passed to the Department for Transport (DfT), but this showed that the key outputs contained in its predecessor's strategy programmes for 2004 and 2005 had been delivered on time. The report states that 'many substantial schemes had been delivered including line speed improvements along the whole route up to 125mph in tilt mode, re-signalling, track and overhead line renewals and improvements, electrification of the Crewe–Kidsgrove line, plus power supply upgrades, new and extended platforms, Nuneaton flyover and new junctions at several locations'.

The DfT acknowledges that the West Coast Main Line is the UK's most important trunk rail route carrying increasing numbers of passengers and around 40 per cent of the country's rail freight. The June 2003 strategy had to address the need to repair and renew the route to ensure continued operation of trains along it and also ensure that it provided the extra capacity and capability needed for fast, long-distance passenger services as well

as continuing to allow for the important local and regional services, together with the ever growing freight market. The 2006 report states a decision was taken that 'Proven technology was to be used wherever possible: the project was on a huge scale and could not continue to be burdened with the uncertainties in timescales and costs associated with the development of new technology'. This was an important decision which played a significant part in reducing the total costs of the upgrade to manageable proportions.

The decision did not mean that no new technology would be used in the upgrade work. Far from it, and the use of axle counters have, after initial problems with software, proved to be reliable. The section of route between Cheadle Hulme and Macclesfield was re-signalled using, new-to-the-UK rail network, 'computer based interlocking' (CBI). This was a relatively simple installation which has shown itself to be thoroughly reliable in service. However, for more complex signalling areas such as that at Stockport, the use of the new technology was considered to have the potential of introducing very high risk that could have a serious impact on the introduction of the September 2004 timetable. As a consequence, the original signalling was thoroughly refurbished, although the track, foundations, drainage and overhead line were all replaced.

The magnitude of the work completed between June 2003 and March 2006 should not be underestimated, and would not have been possible without a step-change from pre-2002, which produced the important, much-needed co-operation from all the industry parties involved. The Department for Transport had now assumed the role of taking on the strategic lead with Network Rail taking the lead in project delivery. The achievements included:

- Line speed improvements throughout the route, including signalling, overhead line modifications and the installation of balises to interface with onboard tilt and speed supervision systems.

- The extensive programme of blockades for through route-wide modernisation.

- Track renewals to correct the inherited backlog and to prepare for the new speeds.

- Overhead line overhaul and renewals.

- Power supply upgrades, with new feeder stations and the successful smooth changeover of the first section of route to the more resilient auto-transformer supply configuration.

- Resignalling schemes, with the first southern stages of the new signalling centre at Rugby being commissioned, and Cheadle Hulme, Colwich and Euxton areas being completed.

- New platforms at Birmingham New Street, Stockport and Wolverhampton plus improved turn-back facilities at Tring, Birmingham International and Wigan.

- Nuneaton – flyover, new signalling, new island platform – and Stockport renewals.

- New junctions at Bourne End, Ledburn and Euxton.

- Freight loading gauge enhancements, including the Crewe and Stoke routes through to Manchester Trafford Park.

- Platform extensions to allow 12-car trains to operate at stations along the route between London and Northampton.

These completed sections of the overall project ensured that the major September 2004 timetable changes could be implemented. They also saw the fastest journey times from Glasgow to London cut by 42 minutes to 4 hours 24 minutes, and Manchester to London down to just 2 hours 6 minutes.

The DfT 2006 report also identifies significant benefits to the economy resulting from improved frequencies, journey times and dependability of services. It states: 'The upgrade has increased the mobility of people in a way that has reduced business time and costs, increased network resilience and encouraged economic development', highlighting the developments in the area around

Manchester Piccadilly station and proposals for major redevelopment of Birmingham New Street and London Euston, to name but a few.

The 2003 strategy programme highlighted the need for additional car parking space at stations along the route. Demand for additional parking goes hand in hand with increasing levels of patronage and will become a problem when the next major change to the West Coast timetable occurs in 2009. Consequently a major review of car parking is under way and a Network Rail/Train Operator joint scheme will provide an additional 5,000 spaces.

The completion of the upgrade in 2008 is huge-

Top: **Pre-formed point-work being lifted into place at Ledburn Junction near Hemel Hempstead.** *railphotolibrary.com*

Above: **Overhead line replacement during the upgrade. The new track and shiny copper wire make a stark contrast to the old LMS road bridge in the background.** *railphotolibrary.com*

Above: **Two generations of tilting trains at Crewe on 16 June 2002 as a new Virgin Pendolino stands alongside the original British Railways Board Advanced Passenger Train.**
Virgin Trains / Milepost 92$^{1/2}$

Left: **Seen in 2001, a Virgin Class 390 Pendolino under assembly at Alstom's Washwood Heath factory in Birmingham.**
Virgin Trains / Milepost 92$^{1/2}$

Below: **Pendolinos under construction at Washwood Heath in 2003.**
Virgin Trains / Milepost 92$^{1/2}$

ly important, but of similar importance is the need to ensure proper maintenance of the route in the future in order to avoid a de-generation of the type that occurred pre-privatisation. The Department for Transport strategy post 2008 includes:

- Installing equipment which has a lower requirement for maintenance, such as heavier rails. Lower maintenance means less requirement for staff on the route infrastructure, particularly during peak time services; this in turn will reduce risk to track and signalling staff and should contribute to further improvements in safety.

- Providing systems to improve ease of maintenance and renewals, such as access points, higher output machines, and track inspection by trains rather than patrols on foot.

- Providing network functionality so that future maintenance and renewal is made easier, such as bi-directional signalling, simplified layouts with adequate spacing between tracks and suitable diversionary routes.

- Reducing the impact on the operation of services, especially at weekends, such as by using different equipment and more closely integrating planning.

Whilst the West Coast Main Line upgrade will not result in a fully renewed route the strategy states that 'it will not lead to a maintenance holiday on completion of the 2002–2008 period of substantially higher levels of engineering works to deliver those renewals and the linked enhancement projects … It will be required not to allow deterioration in the restored asset quality or enhanced outputs'.

Pendolinos

Pendolino tilting trains manufactured by Fiat Ferroviaria had been in service for some ten years on the Italian State Railways and had a good record. They were in fact performing extremely well in eight other European countries, thus providing the opportunity to purchase a train with a proven pedigree. Virgin West Coast entered discussions with the Italian company to consider whether this type of train would be suitable for the busy UK rail network. Some years previously British Rail had itself developed a tilting train (known as the Advanced Passenger Train or APT) for use on the West Coast Main Line, but sadly, although it did run in service very briefly it was not deemed successful enough and the project was cancelled. A survivor can currently be found at the Crewe Railway Heritage Centre.

The Pendolinos (or more correctly Pendolino Britannico, meaning British Tilting Trains) were delivered as eight-car sets and a sensible early

A Pendolino sits on the mobile jacks at Washwood Heath awaiting the fitting of its bogies.
Virgin Trains / Milepost 92$^{1/2}$

decision taken by VT was to increase capacity by including a ninth coach to cope with the additional passenger numbers expected.

In a similar fashion to CrossCountry's Voyagers and Super Voyagers the Class 390 Pendolinos used a combination of overseas and British-based manufacturers for construction. The trains themselves were being designed, fitted out, (the body shells were delivered by road from Italy), and to be maintained by Alstom Transport at its Washwood Heath factory in Birmingham. The tilt technology was provided from the Italian giant Fiat Ferroviaria. Subsequently the alliance between the two manufacturers became complete when Alstom (which also created the French TGV), purchased Fiat Ferroviaria in 2001.

The technical specifications (see Appendix A) were very advanced and Virgin Trains needed to be sure that even though tilting trains had earned a good reputation elsewhere, the builders would be able to come up with a train that would dovetail easily with the heavily used rail network in Britain. To satisfy VT's requirements, Alstom would have to deliver on seven particular technical aspects:

1. Doubling train power: The Pendolino would have to give the utmost performance in acceleration, braking and ride quality. The output of 5.1MW at the rails doubled that of the existing fleet used by West Coast, the Class 87 locomotives achieving 2.5MW at 110mph. Power is transmitted through 12 traction motors with the tractive effort remaining constant right up to 125mph.

2. Regenerative braking: Greater acceleration and speed also requires better braking. The Pendolino regenerates the full 5.1MW at rail power. It was a red-letter day for the Pendolino design on 20 August 2003 when set No 390014 became the first AC-powered Inter-City passenger train in the UK to operate with the re-generative brake when it completed a return test trip from Wolverhampton to London Euston. Subsequently Virgin Trains was able to switch the rest of the fleet to the new system. This is environmentally friendly because the national grid is able to recycle the current returned by the train.

The powerful, 9%g brake is delivered by three braking systems, with the train moving between them automatically when the brake is activated. The re-generative brake is always the first applied, but will convert within one second to rheostatic braking if for any reason the overhead line is not receptive. A good example of this is if the train is passing through a neutral section when a driver applies the brake. The third system is conventional friction disc braking which is perfectly capable of stopping the train from 140mph within the designated distance. The friction brake is always set as the initial default braking system.

3. Tilt: The tilt system was developed by Fiat's Swiss subsidiary SIG and gives both a faster response and lower maintenance costs than those which were already in use in Switzerland. Unlike the failed British Rail APT trains tilt system the type fitted to Pendolinos does not provide 100 per cent compensation for curves because that degree of tilt confuses the human eye/body sense of balance. Instead it is limited to 75 per cent compensation on sharp curves giving an 8 degree tilt. The tilt is much less on gentle curves or if the train is travelling at lower speeds. Passengers do not really notice the tilt even at high speed although from the driver's eye view it is very noticeable, but still does not result in the dreaded tilt travel sickness that passengers experienced with the old APT design.

4. Smart Tilt Control (TASS): The UK loading gauge required major technical changes to the standard for the European continent. Britain's rail safety authorities specified that the default position of tilt control should be 'locked out', with a re-affirmation of tilt command every two miles when in use. The British requirement was also for a speed supervision system to remove the risk of 'over-speed' during tight curves. The system installed on the Pendolino is called Tilt Authorisation and Speed Control (TASS). It was designed as a joint venture between Alstom Signalling and Alstom Transport and will ultimately fit with the ERTMS cab signalling system, when it is fully developed at some stage in the future. Virgin Trains used Pendolino set No 390012 to test the entire TASS package and found it to perform well. Subsequently the entire fleet had its tilt systems upgraded to TASS and all VT's drivers received specialist training to enable the December 2005 timetable to be fully implemented.

5. High Tech Service: Particular attention was given to the passenger areas of the trains. Every seat has an electronic reservation display (as do the Voyager and Super Voyager trains), which is updated instantly when train managers update their computers. Information is downloaded by beaming it from the central reservations system and reservations can be made up to 30 minutes before the train leaves its journey starting point. It is possible for the system to be enabled before the train arrives at its destination so that reservations are shown for the following journey, before it actually arrives at the next starting point if required. This has a major time-saving benefit when compared with the system it replaced when staff had to walk through a train placing printed reservation slips on seat backs – although with a disadvantage in readability for passengers.

Electronic information regarding the train's journey and coach number is shown at every door and on the bulkheads at the end of carriages. These use a GPS tracking system which allows next destination and expected arrival time to be displayed accurately.

The Pendolino carriages were amongst the first on the UK rail network to have closed circuit television (CCTV) installed in every coach. The cameras record to police standards. Every seat on the trains is fitted with its own aircraft-style audio system offering up to 14 channels of live radio, news and recorded music.

6. Safety Case: All trains operating on Britain's rail network have to hold a stringent safety case. In the case of the Pendolino it was particularly exhaustive for three reasons, with these being:

a. It was the first train to include additional European Interoperability Regulation requirements.
b. It had many innovative features such as TASS.
c. The high number of safety groups required to have its certificate; a good example is that the West Coast Main Line ran through three Network Rail Regions, but reduced to two by 2005. At the time of the Pendolino's introduction it was necessary to make the same safety case presentation to each region separately and responses could be, and were, widely differing.

The Pendolino is required to operate on both the newly upgraded infrastructure and the parts which are unmodified. Interface issues such as physical clearances and electrical interference have long been a major headache for the introduction of new trains and for Pendolino it was no different. As a consequence, when interface problems occurred in trial running of the new trains it was automatically assumed that the guilty party was the Pendolino, a sort of guilty without trial. Fortunately, the technical engineers were able to overcome any difficulties and the Pendolino now holds a full safety case certificate for all its areas of operation.

A Pendolino bogie waits to be fitted to its carriage at the Alstom works in 2002.
Virgin Trains / Milepost 92¹/²

7. Train Reliability: The impressive technology would have been of absolutely no value unless it worked fully when in service. For Virgin Trains the consequences of failure in traffic would be quite simply unacceptable. The old stock which the new trains were replacing had a miles per casualty rate of around 6,500 miles but West Coast required the Pendolino to improve this to 35,000 miles between casualties. Alstom committed itself to achieving the required level and at the time of writing the fleet has reached 10,000 miles between casualties, but it is a fact that the delays caused are substantially less than those of the train's predecessors.

The Class 390s should be described as two electric multiple units operating as one, each being able to operate independently, while at the same time having the ability to cross feed the other. Both halves have their own pantograph, traction package and air conditioning. The driver's in-cab computer allows a prompt diagnosis of any problem allowing the driver to switch to alternative configurations, effectively allowing the train to proceed without disruption to its journey.

It was now clear that Virgin Trains had found a train highly suitable for its West Coast franchise and which had the ability to tilt at speeds of 140mph. The Pendolinos started to be delivered in ones and twos followed by the rest of the fleet over the two years leading up to the 'Red Revolution' timetable in September 2004, in order that trains could be tested over high mileages in advance of the timetables implementation. Anyone within the rail industry will know that brand-new designs of trains nearly all arrive with teething problems when they enter service for the first time. The Pendolino proved to be no different, but Virgin Trains customers, having suffered huge disruption to services while the WCML upgrade was being progressed rightly had the high expectations that are associated with the Virgin brand.

Charles Belcher admitted that the first three months in service did not go well, and even Sir Richard Branson commented at the official timetable launch at Euston station, that there may be some problems as the new trains entered service. The teething problems were not major, but failures of the toilets, (which Charles Belcher admitted was his biggest disappointment since joining West Coast Trains, describing the issue as embarrassing), air-conditioning systems and door controls irritated passengers. None of the difficulties caused serious delays, the average being around ten minutes per incident compared to the 70 or so minutes when failures occurred on the older locomotive hauled trains. As Belcher pointed out, if a Class 87 electric locomotive failed in traffic then very often all that could be done was to summon a replacement locomotive.

Curing all these problems, took time. Particularly irritating to all involved was the fact that air-conditioning unit failures were generally due to bad workmanship. Working closely with Alstom, Virgin's West Coast Trains entered into a programme to replace all of the faulty units and introduced software modifications to rectify other faults. It worked, and within three months by January 2005, things were starting to improve dramatically. Performance and reliability has continued to improve and by May 2006 was regularly hitting 90 per cent of trains arriving on time. If these failures had been his biggest disappointment, Charles Belcher is very proud of the relationship which now exists between Virgin Trains, Alstom and Network Rail, describing them as 'trustworthy partners'. He also claimed the improvement in the relationships as being one of the biggest achievements.

Behind the scenes
(West Coast Trains Ltd)

So what was it like behind the scenes and just how difficult was it in practice to bring the new trains into revenue earning service? An in-depth interview with Chris Green provided the answer. He revealed details that were never in the public eye and explained how, whenever one problem was overcome another stepped in to replace it, at times placing the entire project in doubt.

Sir Richard Branson has always been clear that Virgin Trains would evolve through three phases. The first was to win the franchises; the second was the transitional stage where the railway was kept running while the gigantic projects were delivered, and the third was the 'Quiet Enjoyment' where stability returned and Virgin could do what it did best – marketing a growth business.

So let's have a close look behind the scenes at the complexity which faced Chris Green and his new team when they arrived to implement the second phase.

New trains

Chris Green was chosen in 1999 to lead Virgin Trains through the second, transitional stage, because it was clearly going to need railway experience and teamwork across the industry. It was recognised that renewing the entire train fleets of both franchises over a four-year period would create a huge strain on management resources. In theory, new trains should work 'out of the box' in the way a new car does. The reality is that every new train fleet tends to be bespoke with untried technology sitting amongst the traditional products. There are very few examples in the UK of evolutionary development of new trains. Freight perhaps offers the best example, with the continuous evolution from Class 59 to the now-standard Class 66 freight locomotives from long Canadian production lines. They really do work out of the box when unloaded from the ship.

Virgin Trains did not have this luxury on either its CrossCountry or West Coast franchises. It was rightly looking for revolution rather than evolution. It didn't want more of the same; it wanted a 140mph tilting electric train for West Coast and 125mph diesel trains for CrossCountry, some of which would also need to tilt. This meant accepting some technology risk in order to give passengers a boost in speed and comfort.

Virgin Trains recognised the technical risks right from the beginning and created a powerful Major Projects Team which managed not only the building and testing of the new trains, but also the complex interfaces with Railtrack/Network Rail for the improved infrastructure – not to mention the ever-more demanding safety cases.

The plague of locusts

The new team knew that they faced some unknowns, but nobody could have foreseen the level of unplanned events that were to be thrown at them. As Chris Green said: 'We were hit by every conceivable disaster short of the proverbial plague of locusts in those five years.' These problems fell into two broad categories: technical show stoppers and financial disasters – and both appeared on epic scales that would have destroyed many projects.

Financial locusts

Taking the financial challenges first, just about every partner in the West Coast story hit some form of financial meltdown in the period of the project – and yet this giant project will still be delivered, albeit about two years late. The biggest blow came when Railtrack, the central player in funding and implementing the 140mph infrastructure upgrade, was forced into Railway Administration in 2002 – effectively bankrupted by the Hatfield track fiasco, the mountain of compensation that arose from it, and the difficulties the company faced in trying to honour the PUG 2 contract. The period of Railtrack in Railway Administration that followed left the project on drip feed and in a parlous state with the future unknown with funding, and hence project delivery, kept to a minimum. Then, another learning curve occurred when Network Rail took the project over and finally brought stability, commitment and delivery from 2003.

But Virgin Trains also lost its financial stability when Railtrack fell ill. It was, dependent on Railtrack both for track upgrades which would allow its new trains to earn their income – and for compensation totalling up to £250 million for infrastructure delivery failures. The result was that Virgin Trains also went onto government drip feed from July 2002, operating under letters of agreement with the Strategic Rail Authority. This was effectively a supplement to the franchise agreement, where it remained totally committed to the project, but from which it would not emerge with a re-negotiated franchise agreement until December 2006.

The difference in the West Coast letter of

agreement though, was that because it did not include the 'no fault termination' clause, contained in the CrossCountry version. Virgin West Coast could have continued to run the franchise through to 2012 under the original terms even if it had been unable to reach agreement with the Department for Transport, which has taken over responsibility for Britain's railways from the Strategic Rail Authority. However, as Tony Collins told the author, it should be remembered that at no stage did the SRA flinch in allowing the new trains to be ordered, and they were ably supported by Sir Richard Branson who agreed that the Pendolinos should receive a ninth carriage. Both deserve credit for those decisions.

The next meltdown concerned Alstom, which was not only contracted to build the Pendolino fleet, but also to maintain it until 2012. They were ripped apart in a financial restructuring in 2003 after overreaching themselves at global level which saw the French government become a 28 per cent shareholder. There was a real fear that they would shut down all production in the UK and attempt to transfer the Pendolino production line to Spain in mid-build. In the event, the closure was delayed until the last Pendolino was delivered, but huge disruption took place in Alstom UK behind the scenes as factories closed, organisations adapted, and project teams changed endlessly.

And finally, the Strategic Rail Authority, which had rescued the West Coast upgrade so effectively from the jaws of defeat when Railtrack collapsed found itself closed down two years later, in 2005. The SRA had been a major force in supporting the West Coast modernisation and it was a relief when the process of transferring its knowledge and leadership to the Department for Transport proved to be straightforward, thus avoiding yet another destabilising of the project.

In summary, it is quite astonishing that all the major players in the West Coast project could have taken such hard body blows in the two years from 2002 to 2004 and yet stayed committed to working together to keep the project alive.

Technical locusts

And that was just the 'financial locusts'; the swarm of 'technical locusts' was just as bad – and came at the same time. As Chris Green says: 'The West Coast upgrade happened against all the odds because we all developed a wartime determination to deliver the mission.'

140mph infrastructure lost

The most high-profile technical challenge was Railtrack's announcement in December 1999 that it could not deliver the radical 'moving block' signalling that had been proposed. This was an important issue for both 140mph running and the entire re-signalling of the West Coast Main Line. This, together with the Hatfield issues, was at the centre of Railtrack's subsequent collapse. Good news often flows from evil, however, and one

result of the financial meltdown, was that Railtrack in Railway Administration started working much more closely with Virgin Trains and the newly formed Strategic Rail Authority. This led to the more realistic plans for 125mph tilting trains by 2004, but left the Pendolino interfacing with an old infrastructure which was to prove challenging. For example, it quickly emerged that Railtrack did not have a comprehensive knowledge of its assets and the effect they would have on a high-technology tilting train, whether it was signalling interface or the gauging of track, bridges, tunnels and platforms. All of these were in the 'start again' box.

High-tech trains
on low-tech infrastructure

The Pendolino was designed as a high-tech train running on new high-tech infrastructure. In the event, it had to be introduced on an old railway with much of the signalling and overhead electrification equipment dating back half a century, with very little less than 30 years old. This was bound to produce a whole new range of problems, and it did. First, it was a tilting train running on a railway where Robert Stephenson, Joseph Locke and their colleagues had most certainly not designed the bridges and clearances for trains to tilt.

Secondly, it was an electric train drawing 25,000 volts from the overhead catenary and returning this to the running rails. Its state-of-the-art electronic control equipment had to avoid any interference with the signalling systems.

Thirdly, it was designed to use electric braking which involved 'reversing' the electric motors and sending large spikes of electric current back to adjacent tracks and sub stations for re-use.

The initial reaction on both sides was to seek protection behind their legal contracts. It quickly became clear however, that the technical issues

Sir Richard Branson is unable to hide his delight with the new Pendolino trains.
Virgin Trains / Milepost 92$^{1/2}$

were so complex that the choice lay between years of legal wrangling or pooling resources 'without prejudice to future compensation'. To everyone's eternal credit, a joint meeting was held in January 2002 at which it was decided to pool resources and work as a joint team.

The new group was called Pendolino into Traffic and quickly became known as PIT. The new PIT team sought to create a 'command and control' structure in a deeply fragmented railway. It met every week for three years almost without exception and it remorselessly ensured that every technical obstacle to introduction was listed and solved – regardless of ownership. PIT was jointly chaired by Chris Green as Chief Executive of Virgin Trains and Tom McCarthy as West Coast Project Director for Network Rail. With them were senior directors from Alstom Trains, Alstom Signalling, Angel Trains and the Strategic Rail Authority.

The Commonwealth Games 2002

The first target was to get a Pendolino into service for the Commonwealth Games in Manchester in June 2002. This sporting challenge proved the ideal target to galvanise a group of competing teams into a single project. From that point, PIT started to become a single team.

The Commonwealth Games target brought a whole series of technical issues to a head. It was already clear that the tilt mechanism would remain locked out of use until the West Coast could be gauge cleared. Such was the lack of asset knowledge, that the entire route had to be measured by hand every few metres to record the precise location of track, bridges, platforms and tunnels. This exercise identified the areas that were judged to be too tight for tilting trains to pass at speed and these were progressively cleared in a seemingly endless series of additional engineering possessions.

Red Revolution

The next priority was to re-establish the credibility of using a tilting train in Britain. Alstom had bought a ten-mile test track at Asfordby near Melton Mowbray, and the Pendolinos were being hammered up and down this to get reliability experience. Chris Green saw his opportunity and persuaded Alstom to invite the press to Asfordby to demonstrate the Pendolino at 125mph in tilting mode.

Being Virgin Trains, the event mushroomed into a major VIP occasion which became known as 'Red Revolution Day'. Red for the new trains, even though the new livery was predominantly silver, and revolution for the highly technical trains they heralded. A huge media and rail industry party filled an eight-car Voyager from London's St Pancras station in June 2002 and the special train took guests straight onto the test track at Melton Mowbray and into the test depot where the world saw the Voyager and Pendolino side by side for the first time.

Guests were taken into a marquee next to the test track for a briefing by Sir Richard Branson, which dramatically climaxed with the marquee being revolved complete with guests, exactly as the test Pendolino burst out of the tunnel at full tilt. The sight was dramatic and to add to the excitement, the Red Arrows performed a fly past over the tunnel exactly as the train exited.

The day was completed with demonstration runs on the tilting Pendolino, with the media becoming the first Pendolino passengers in Britain. Chris Green was heard to say: 'The Red Revolution event restored public faith in the tilting Pendolinos, and the media became more supportive from that day.'

Eager to show off its sleek new super-train, Virgin West Coast provided Pendolino No 390043 *Virgin Explorer* to star at the 2004 Railfest held by the National Railway Museum in York. The train was on display between 29 May and 6 June 2004, with some 60,000 visitors taking the opportunity to view Britain's most modern train. In addition a draw was made for a specially-commissioned model Pendolino (No 390200 *Pen y Darren*) and limited-edition wagons, which saw the Yorkshire Ambulance service benefit to the tune of £4434.34.

Electrical interference

The next problem was the sheer power of the Pendolino. There was a fear that electrical demand could damage the overhead power supply, so dampers had to be fitted to the 25kV catenary every 30 miles to protect the system. This meant not just more engineering possessions, but a severe limit on the number of Pendolinos that could operate in any section of the route – down to one train only in some cases.

Finally, the gauge clearance and dampers allowed the first test trains to start running in the London area, and this led to a critical night test at Euston when four Pendolinos left the station simultaneously to test the impact on signalling and power supplies. All was well – and this led to the famous picture of the first Pendolinos lined up by their drivers for a midnight photo call at Wembley depot. Even so, it was to be another two years before the full Pendolino fleet could operate without restriction.

Signalling interference

Then a new bombshell dropped in the shape of signalling interference. As the Pendolino accelerated and braked it transmitted a series of electronic signals which were designed to avoid interfering with the lineside equipment. However, the early tests for the Commonwealth Games deadline showed that Pendolinos were in fact interfering with signalling cables and relays at a small number of locations.

This could have been the beginning of some very expensive counter-suing as both parties sought to prove that their equipment was 'work-

Accompanied by pretty girls, Sir Richard Branson and Brian Souter celebrate the coming of the Pendolinos. *Virgin Trains*

ing to specification'. Instead, Pendolino into Traffic proved its worth and the teams agreed to address the technical issues as a joint problem. Alstom found a quick fix which eliminated the most harmful frequency from the Pendolino fleet. The modified train was then run to act as a fault finder for the remaining problem sites. Virtually every site needed a tailored solution and it rapidly became clear that it would not be possible to clear the London–Manchester route in time for the Commonwealth Games.

Tom McCarthy, West Coast Route Modernisation Director for Network Rail, then entered into the spirit of the new teamwork and volunteered to clear the Birmingham–Manchester route for the Pendolino in time for the Games. And so it was that No 390010 became the first Pendolino to run in passenger service into Manchester in June 2002, seen on live television, where it was met by Sir Richard Branson and named *Commonwealth Games 2002*, by the Lord Mayor of Manchester. Chris Green remembers today that 'it was worth every minute of the stress: and from that point PIT became one team determined to up its game'.

Timetable challenge: September 2004
The Commonwealth Games was only the hors d'oeuvre compared to the next challenge which came from the Strategic Rail Authority. Richard Bowker, (SRA Chairman), had now taken strategic management of the West Coast Project from a failed Railtrack and made a public commitment that the full West Coast tilting timetable would be introduced by September 2004. This bold move proved to be the critical factor in forcing all parties to make common cause in solving the gigantic problems that remained ahead. It also ensured that the equally gigantic investment funding remained underwritten by government and the newly arrived Network Rail.

Chris Green is positive over the role the Strategic Rail Authority played in keeping the West Coast upgrade on track in those difficult years. He recognises that Richard Bowker personally championed the need to complete the upgrade with government, and fought for the additional funding. Stuart Baker, previously with Northern Spirit, was appointed by the SRA to spearhead the upgrade and mastermind the co-ordination of the new timetable, with the authority to juggle other operator's train services to fit the plan.

The first Pendolino in revenue-earning service, complete with Commonwealth Games 'Gold Medal', stands alongside one of its Voyager cousins at Manchester Piccadilly in June 2002. *Peter W. Robinson*

Four Pendolinos lined up by their drivers for an impromptu photo-shoot at Wembley after the successful completion of night trials at Euston station in March 2002.
Virgin Trains

A shot of the speedometer during a night test run in August 2002 when a Pendolino reached 145mph between Rugby and Nuneaton.
Virgin Trains / Milepost 92¹ᐟ²

The newly created Network Rail was galvanised into delivering a detailed plan to clear all the sites where signalling and cable interference were preventing the Pendolinos running – 'without prejudice to whether the problem lay with train or signalling'. This realistic decision ignored the contractual disputes and accepted that whatever the rights and wrongs, this was the only way a quick fix for the problem would be found. It saved the day and involved a massive re-routing of cable services between Crewe and Scotland. These changes also ended the limits on how many Pendolinos could operate in any particular area and allowed the powerful electric braking systems to be introduced.

Aerodynamics

Then one of the endless Safety Cases raised the issue of aerodynamics and the risk of a tilting Pendolino overturning in a high gust of wind. This issue had been addressed in the train design following experience in other countries, but computer simulation suggested that the line over Shap Fell was a special case that needed to be recognised. A team solution was found that involved ballasting the lighter end car of the Pendolino (the one without the kitchen), providing additional wind protection at exposed sites and introducing wind speed recorders that automatically trigger line speed reductions in extreme circumstances. The Pendolino fleet was modified for high wind performance in time for the September 2004 timetable. The recent derailment of a Japanese non-tilt train in high wind conditions is a reminder that the issue is indeed real.

Diversionary routes

The West Coast Main Line is the third busiest route in Europe and runs round the clock with heavy freight trains filling the night hours that engineers would otherwise traditionally use. Major engineering work can only be achieved by closing complete sections of the route at weekends and diverting passenger services. The realisation that the 363 days per year guaranteed access to the West Coast Main Line for Pendolinos in service, mentioned earlier was unrealistic, meant that the electric Pendolino trains had to be hauled over non-electrified diversions by diesel locomotives which were compatible with the new, sophisticated tilting trains. Even worse, it meant that the diversionary routes had to undergo the dreaded gauging process in their turn to ensure they were compatible with the new Pendolino profile, even though its tilt mechanism would be locked out of use. Both tasks proved to be daunting.

Virgin Trains decided to purchase and modify a fleet of twelve Class 47 locomotives to act as 'Thunderbirds' for hauling Pendolinos off the wire. This number was increased to 16 when the scale of the problem was realised and these became Class 57/3. The interface between the locomotives and the Pendolinos proved to be far more complex than was first anticipated. A compromise was found for the September 2004 timetable, but it left a legacy of slow and complex locomotive changes on the scheduled Virgin West Coast North Wales services as well as the weekend diversions. However, by 2006 improvements had been made which saw dwell times at Crewe only six minutes longer than using a standard locomotive and train sets – a small price to pay for the vital extra capacity over the previously planned use of a four-car Class 221 Super Voyager because the North Wales route is a high-performance part of the West Coast service.

The gauging of the more northerly diversionary routes for hauled Pendolinos proved very time consuming and expensive. It took almost a year to clear the diversion via Bolton because of very low flying arches at Chorley. It also cost millions of pounds to get clearance under the numerous low bridges on the Kilmarnock, Glasgow and South Western diversion north of Carlisle and this was only completed in 2005. With its single-line sections, and heavy coal traffic, capacity is also an issue on this route and passengers often found themselves on replacement road coaches in the meantime.

High-speed testing

Angel Trains, the ultimate owner of the Pendolino fleet, was rightly insistent that Alstom should demonstrate that the trains were capable of running at their design speed of 140mph. A night test run was held between Rugby and Nuneaton in August 2002 where the train effortlessly accelerated to 145mph and braked equally impressively. Chris Green told the author that 'It rode beautifully and we actually had to shut the power off at 145mph. The most impressive features were the ride quality at high speed and the electric brake which brought the train to a stand in just over one signal section.'

Pendolino modifications

The high-speed tests were the clinching evidence that the Pendolino trains are fundamentally an excellent product. The problem was that it could not run high mileages at high speeds to de-bug any design problems, because there was just not enough 125mph tilt-enabled track available until September 2004. A few trains were programmed to run higher mileages and this was just enough to identify a suite of reliability modifications which would have to be applied to the fleet that was still being built. The bugs were almost all electronic and had to go through complex safety cases of their own. These included modifications to the suspension, tilt package and the blending of the complex electric/air braking.

The race was now on to modify the remaining 52 Pendolinos in time for the September 2004 timetable date. Some were done on the production line but others had to be withdrawn from

service for up to a month at a time for all the outstanding work to be completed. The final result was 42 Pendolinos modified and available for the new timetable, with the remainder due to be completed by the end of that year.

From a train that could barely achieve 2,000 miles between faults, the Pendolino by 2006 was five times better at 10,000 miles and rising but still a long way short of the required 35,000 miles. Fleet engineers often say that you can tell a good train from its first day on the tracks and the Pendolino has always felt like a good train technically. It has rarely failed on the mainline and most faults can be quickly resolved by simply shutting the systems down and rebooting the 200 or so computers on board, just like a domestic computer. The stroke of genius was to design the Pendolino as effectively two electrically independent trains coupled together. The level of redundancy is so high (e.g. two pantographs, two transformers and twelve traction motors), that Britain's most complex train is also set to become its most reliable.

25 September 2004 –
Tilting timetable launch

The PIT team finally got its reward for two years of hard labour behind the scenes at 10.30 on Thursday, 25 September 2004, when Sir Richard Branson escorted the Prime Minister, Tony Blair, onto London's Euston station to a triumphant scene. There were rows of shining, fully modified Pendolinos to greet him, the entire rail industry seemed to be represented, including Richard Bowker, and above all there were several young Virgin Trains staff in their bright red uniforms signifying the new generation.

Chris Green was able to announce the end of the transition phase and his pride in being able to hand over an upgraded railway to his successor Tony Collins was obvious to all present. Collins had

Prime Minister Tony Blair makes a speech welcoming the high-speed Pendolino service in September 2004 in the presence of Sir Richard Branson and several Virgin Trains staff.
Virgin Trains / Milepost 92$^{1/2}$

Virgin Trains Chief Executive, Chris Green, greets the Prime Minister, Tony Blair, at Euston station in September 2004, watched by Sir Richard Branson and joyous Virgin staff at the launch of the Pendolino high-speed service on the upgraded West Coast Main Line.
Peter W. Robinson

One of Virgin West Coast's Pendolino trains stands on the inspection pit at Manchester's Longsight depot on 11 May 2005.
Stuart Baker

previously been Virgin Trains Director Major Projects and Deputy Chief Executive, doing so much to keep the all-important contracts and negotiations alive through this very difficult period.

Then came the exciting moment for all Virgin Trains people when No 390029 *City of Stoke-on-Trent* was ceremoniously flagged away by the Prime Minister for a non-stop run to Manchester. When asked to guess the likely journey time, Sir Richard Branson said: 'two hours would be great'. In fact driver Tommy Farr brought No 390029 to a stand in the platform at Manchester Piccadilly station in just one hour and fifty three minutes – and then repeated the feat on the return run to Euston. Both the Pendolino and the infrastructure had performed to perfection with 125mph tilt giving an effortless average speed of 101mph. The transition period was indeed over and the marketing era had arrived. In Chris Green's words: 'an era has arrived in which rail must surely triumph over short-haul airlines at last.'

As was the case with the introduction of CrossCountry's Voyagers and Super Voyagers, Virgin Trains embarked on a programme of naming each of the Class 390 trains. The word

'Pendolino' was included in the trains' red nameplates because it was unfamiliar in the UK and needed this daily 'sales campaign' to ensure that it became part of the language. Many of the trains have been named after the cities they serve on the West Coast route network.

The Central Rivers experience, referred to later in this book, exposes the long-term weakness in West Coast's Pendolino fleet, which never got its purpose-built mother depot and is split between a number of 19th century depots which have been modified to various degrees. Ultimately, the fleet must benefit from the provision of a specialist Pendolino maintenance base to ensure consistently high levels of reliability. Alstom holds the maintenance contract for the Pendolino fleet until 2012 and continued to do so after it closed its manufacturing premises in the Washwood Heath suburb of Birmingham. The company retained much of the management experience it would require to fulfil the contract by transferring managers to some of the depots. The main beneficiary was Longsight depot in Manchester, but a supporting staff was also retained at Oxley, near Wolverhampton.

On 24 March 2006, Alstom opened its new Control Centre at the West Coast Traincare Centre at Longsight and teams are based there for all aspects of Pendolino maintenance. Some work is also carried out at the new centre for other train operators. Virgin's West Coast franchise requires 46 Pendolinos to be available every day in order to fulfil its service obligations, and with the increasing reliability of the new trains is consistently meeting this target. Whilst it is not exactly a mother ship in the same sense as Central Rivers is to the Voyager and Super Voyager fleet, it is well equipped and includes a new bogie repair shop. Larger premises are still needed though, and the company is moving part of its operation across the running lines and into the former Regional Eurostar International

Depot. At the time of writing that depot is occupied by Siemens where it bases its Class 185 operations. However, Siemens is moving to a purpose-built depot near Manchester at Ardwick, and when that is complete Alstom will be able to occupy the former International Depot. This is important because the Pendolino fleet is to undergo a programme to fit sanding equipment – a project due to take up to six months to complete in 2006.

Further investment by Alstom in its maintenance operation includes:

▨ A bogie drop facility at Polmadie depot in Scotland.

▨ New office facilities, new pitted road with a bogie drop, and single-vehicle paint shop at Oxley.

▨ New wheel drop facilities at Wembley.

▨ Heating and air conditioning repair facilities at Edge Hill near Liverpool.

The new Control Centre was opened by Tony Collins who commented that it was now time to look upon the Pendolino as an 'old train with passengers expecting them to be turned out to very highest standards every day.'

Whilst at just two years old, the Pendolino cannot literally be considered to be an old train, the message is clear that passengers are now used to seeing them in service every day and West Coast would prefer the days of the old fleet which they replaced to remain in the dim and distant past. At present though they still make occasional appearances when the Pendolinos return to depot for modifications.

Top: **Pendolino No 390045 stands at Manchester Piccadilly station on 27 September 2004.** *Stuart Baker*

Above: **A brand-new Pendolino pauses at Crewe on its way to Scotland in 2003.** *John Balmforth*

Above left: **A Virgin Pendolino races down Grayrigg bank in the Lakeland Fells through a heavy rain storm with a south bound train in 2003.** *Stuart Baker*

Three Pendolinos stand side-by-side at Manchester Piccadilly following the high-speed run by No 390029 on 17 September 2004. The train completed the journey from London in 1 hour 53 minutes.
Stuart Baker

A Pendolino works its way through Penrith with a northbound service on a very wet day in 2004. The foot-crossing is the only means of accessing the island platform for wheelchair-bound passengers.
Virgin Trains / Milepost 92$^{1/2}$

Above: **West Coast Pendolino and CrossCountry Super Voyager rest between turns at Manchester Piccadilly in August 2002.** *Virgin Trains / Milepost 92¹/²*

Left: **A gleaming new Pendolino waits at Euston station alongside one of the loco-hauled Mk 3 and DVT train sets the Pendolinos will replace.** *Virgin Trains / Milepost 92¹/²*

Behind the scenes conclusion

Chris Green summed up the West Coast achievement in an interview after the great launch event. 'We are standing here today for two reasons. First, because Virgin had the sense to create some really professional contracts between a wide range of partners. Secondly, because when the going became tough, it also had the sense to park the contracts and enter into a close teamwork with its partners to get the job delivered for the nation. Tony Collins and I symbolise those two phases. He was the guru on contracts and I was able to concentrate on developing teamwork. We made a good team and I wish him every success as West Coast enters the marketing phase at last.'

At the time of writing, in 2006, as we watch the tilting Pendolinos flash round the reverse curves at Berkhamsted at 125mph, and as we applaud punctuality levels which are routinely at 90 per cent or better, there is a need to reflect and remember that the years of unseen teamwork between partners from widely differing organisations made it all possible.

Above: **A Euston–Wolverhampton service passes a narrow boat on the Oxford Canal near Anstey in 2003.**
Virgin Trains / Milepost 92$^{1/2}$

Right: **One of Virgin West Coast's Pendolino trains awaits departure at Birmingham New Street with a London Euston to Wolverhampton service on 23 April 2005. A Central Trains service waits alongside with a service to Walsall.** *Michael Hughes*

Below right: **A Pendolino tilts its way through a curve at Great Strickland on another miserable wet day.**
Virgin Trains / Milepost 92$^{1/2}$

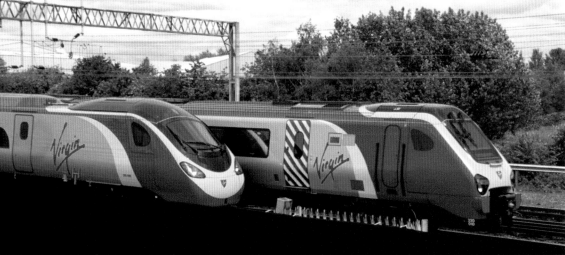

Above: **A new Pendolino is hauled off wire under the flying arches at Chorley as it undergoes gauge clearance testing in 2002.**
Virgin Trains / Milepost 92¹/²

Left: **A West Coast Pendolino and a CrossCountry Voyager pass outside the Heritage Centre at Crewe.**
Virgin Trains / Milepost 92¹/²

Below left: **A Virgin Pendolino on the Alstom test track at Old Dalby in 2002.**
Virgin Trains / Milepost 92¹/²

Left: The first inter-city service to display an all-over advertising livery saw Pendolino No 390029 *City of Stoke-on-Trent* carry advertising for a new 'Superman' film in 2006. *Virgin Trains*

Below: Looking like an exotic caterpillar, the 'Superman'-liveried No 390029 heads north near Milnthorpe. *Donald Burgess*

Right: A Virgin Super Voyager heads along the North Wales coast at Penmaenmawr with a train from Holyhead in August 2004.
Virgin Trains / Milepost 92¹ᐟ²

Top: **A Super Voyager on a West Coast service to Holyhead passes the medieval ramparts of Conway Castle in North Wales during August 2004.** *Virgin Trains / Milepost 92¹ᐟ²*

Above: **The first working of the 11.21 Euston–Llandudno with a Super Voyager eases through Deganwy in September 2004.** *Virgin Trains / Milepost 92¹ᐟ²*

Right: **Virgin West Coast's 'Thunderbird' Class 57/3 diesel-electric locomotive No 57312** *The Hood* **stands at Rugby awaiting its next call to duty on 15 March 2006.** *John Balmforth*

Above: **A pair of Class 57 'Thunderbirds' pilot a Pendolino across the marshes at Rhosnieger, Anglesey with a Holyhead to London Euston train in September 2004.** *Virgin Trains / Milepost 92$^{1/2}$*

Right: **Class 57/3 No 57301** *Scott Tracy* **on 'Thunderbird' duty hauling a Pendolino along the West Coast Main Line.** *Virgin Trains / Milepost 92$^{1/2}$*

Below right: **Another 'Thunderbird' locomotive heads a diverted train past Clitheroe Castle in 2004.** *Virgin Trains / Milepost 92$^{1/2}$*

Above: **Class 57/3 No 57307** *Lady Penelope* **in action, deputising for the rostered locomotive, speeds along the West Coast Main Line with a West Coast service.** *Virgin Trains / Milepost 92$^{1/2}$*

Right: **The newly named** *Heaven's Angels*, **Pendolino No 390047, departs Glasgow Central on 22 September 2006 at the start of its record-breaking run to London Euston. The train covered the 401 miles in 3 hours 55 minutes 27 seconds at an average speed of 102.38mph.** *John Balmforth*

West Coast record-breaking run

On 22 September 2006 Pendolino No 390047, newly named *Heaven's Angels*, departed Glasgow Central station at 12.37 for London Euston at the start of an attempt to make the fastest ever southbound rail journey along the West Coast Main Line between the two cities. Preston-based driver Russell Southworth brought the train to a stand at Euston station at 16.32 having completed the journey in a record 3 hours 55 minutes and 27 seconds at an average speed of 102.4mph. The author was privileged to be on-board and as it entered the platform the train's horn was sounded in triumph, accompanied by huge applause from its four hundred passengers. A detailed list of the timings scheduled and achieved is shown at Appendix E.

The trip, sponsored jointly by Virgin Trains and *The Railway Magazine* raised in excess of £36,000 for the Heaven's Angels charity which provides specially adapted motorbikes used by health workers to deliver medical aid to remote areas of Africa.

Left: **Passenger Andy Balmforth eagerly studies the anticipated timing schedule for the record-breaking run by No 390047 from Glasgow Central to London Euston along the West Coast Main Line on 22 September 2006.** *John Balmforth*

CrossCountry:
a brief description

The CrossCountry routes are far more complex than the West Coast route. The latter is essentially a route connecting London and Scotland and serving the large cities *en route*, while those of CrossCountry quite literally serve almost the full length of Britain. Today, CrossCountry still operates through services between Aberdeen and Penzance. Like the West Coast Main Line the CrossCountry routes were not built as a complete entity, but evolved gradually by the mergers of several railway companies. The early CrossCountry services began with the forming of two famous railway companies, the Stockton & Darlington Railway and the Liverpool & Manchester Railway although neither company served London and really did run 'across the country' on an east-west axis. Despite this, neither is part of today's CrossCountry network.

British Rail adopted the use of the 'InterCity' brand for its long-distance quality services in 1966 and CrossCountry's services included the North East/South West route, which was seen to have high potential. This was found to be the case and in 1969 the route was added officially to the InterCity network. It is still an extremely popular and busy route today with both CrossCountry's leisure and business customers.

The introduction of the May 1972 timetable saw an important change for Birmingham with that city finding itself at the hub of the CrossCountry network of services. Crucially routes radiated from North to South via an X shape, with Birmingham at the centre, an arrangement which still exists more than 30 years later. By 1994, CrossCountry ran 10.3 million miles every year over its 1,700 route miles. Possibly its best known train was the 'Cornishman' covering the 704 miles between Dundee and Penzance. The company ran 104 trains carrying in excess of 35,000 passengers daily, with direct services to over 100 stations.

Each of CrossCountry's fleet of 23 High Speed Trains (HSTs) averaged 200,000 miles per year with the maintenance carried out at 19 depots. Additionally, a number of services consisted of Mk 2 carriages hauled by Class 47 diesel-electric locomotives or Class 86 AC electric locomotives. Then, as today, the hub of the CrossCountry network was Birmingham's New Street station. This was the inheritance which passed to Virgin Trains when CrossCountry was privatised.

Evening at Birmingham New Street station, the hub of the Virgin CrossCountry network, on 3 September 2004.
Virgin Trains / Milepost 92$^{1/2}$

Virgin CrossCountry
(CrossCountry Trains Ltd)

Virgin's CrossCountry Trains Limited took control of the franchise with effect from 5 January 1997 just a couple of months before its sister company took on the West Coast franchise. Whereas most of West Coast's locomotive stock was electric the CrossCountry franchise inherited ageing diesel and electric locomotives, elderly carriages and High Speed Train sets which were themselves approaching their third decade. In typical Virgin fashion the first train to be operated on the first day of the CrossCountry franchise was resplendent in the livery of the new operator, this being a Dundee to Penzance service.

CrossCountry had long been regarded as the 'Cinderella' of the InterCity network receiving old trains that no longer had a use elsewhere on the rail network and generally suffering from very little investment. In looking for a reason why this was allowed to happen Chris Green felt that CrossCountry had tried to survive as a regional network within an industry that was obsessed with serving London. Its mission had been to connect the regions of the United Kingdom together and therefore lacked the high profile of the radial routes into the capital city. Green fur-

ther adds that since privatisation CrossCountry has emerged with a new strategic significance as Britain's only national Train Operator. Its goal had to be to provide the link between 18 fragmented train companies, and some 40 per cent of CrossCountry's passengers actually began their journey on other operators' trains. Virgin Trains' job was to transform CrossCountry from 'Cinderella' into a 'Princess'.

Many of CrossCountry's trains travel almost

Above: **Now privately owned, former Virgin Trains Class 47 No 47829 received a special Police livery as part of a 'keep off the rails' safety campaign. It is seen at Crewe on 20 March 2006.**
John Balmforth

Left: **Virgin CrossCountry Class 86 No 86248** *Sir Clwyd/County of Clwyd* **and a rake of Mk 2 coaches wait at Stafford.**
Virgin Trains / Milepost 92$^{1/2}$

Above: **On hire to Virgin CrossCountry, EWS Class 67 locomotive No 67002** departs from Paignton hauling a rake of former Virgin Trains Mk 3 coaching stock on hire to CrossCountry with a summer Saturday service in July 2004.
Virgin Trains / Milepost 92$^{1/2}$

Right: **CrossCountry Class 86 No 86233** in heritage blue livery and carrying its original running number E3172, crosses one of the numerous canals along the route of the West Coast Main Line heading a CrossCountry service.
Virgin Trains / Milepost 92$^{1/2}$

the length of Britain, serving larger towns and cities but, working with other train operators they also provide services for local communities often requiring short-distance travel for daily journeys to and from work, school and college. Such passengers can be found every weekday on CrossCountry trains from Penzance to Plymouth, Banbury to Reading, Congleton to Manchester, Penrith to Carlisle, Chester-le-Street to Newcastle and Dunbar to Edinburgh, but without doubt CrossCountry's busiest train in this respect is the 06.40 service from Dundee to Plymouth. As this train crosses the well known landmark of the Forth Bridge before 08.00 it will already have more than 300 passengers on board travelling from stations in Fife to work in Edinburgh. Other CrossCountry services regularly provide commuter transport into regional centres such as Birmingham, Sheffield, Edinburgh, Oxford and Bristol. All of this shows the strategic importance of the CrossCountry network.

In some urban areas the use of the CrossCountry services by short-distance commuters has caused crowding problems. This has been partly caused by passengers who have alternative local trains provided by other operators, but who choose to travel on the first train to arrive, this often being the Virgin train. Certainly, in and around the West Midlands, this has been the case and has resulted in some long-distance customers not being able to board their required service. In conjunction with the Strategic Rail Authority other operators have

provided extra capacity for local travellers thus easing the pressure on the heavily used CrossCountry services.

As with the West Coast franchise, Virgin Trains made a commitment not only to completely replace the old stock with brand-new trains, but also to attain the enhanced speeds at which the new trains were capable of travelling. Virgin's vision was to deliver 'world-class' travel by 2003. As part of this commitment Railtrack was required to upgrade the CrossCountry routes. In return VT felt confident it would be able to achieve the reduction of the £112.9 million government subsidy to CrossCountry in 1997/98 to zero by 2009/10. Despite the fall of Railtrack it did oversee the CrossCountry routes upgrade to

Below: **Gleaming in its freshly painted heritage blue, No E3172 (86233), newly named** *Alstom Heritage* **stands at Willesden depot on 24 June 2002.**
Virgin Trains / Milepost 92$^{1/2}$

Bottom: **Preston station with a Class 47-hauled Virgin CrossCountry service in 2001.**
Virgin Trains / Milepost 92$^{1/2}$

A splendid array of Class 47 locomotives repainted in heritage liveries, stand in company with a sister loco in Virgin's 'Kit-Kat' colours at Old Oak Common depot.
Virgin Trains / Milepost 92¹ᐟ²

a successful completion in late 2002, although in some cases with lower than anticipated line speeds. CrossCountry services cover some 5,300 service miles and the completion of the upgrade of some 300 miles of track and signalling resulted in the new train fleet being able to operate at speeds in excess of 100mph over two-thirds of its route miles. Some examples of the increased maximum line speeds are:

- 125mph Birmingham–York
- 125mph Wolverhampton–Stafford
- 120mph Birmingham–Bristol/Taunton
- 115mph Birmingham–Solihull/Didcot

Virgin Trains contributed £80 million towards the upgrade package through increased access charges in order to reflect the upgrade investment.

The fleet of trains inherited by Virgin Trains with the CrossCountry franchise were:

Type	Number of vehicles	Year built
Class 47 diesel locomotives	31	1965 to '67
Class 86 electric locomotives	16	1965 to '66
Mk 2 coaches	25 sets	1973 to '76
High Speed Trains	23 x 7-car sets	1982
Class 158 DMUs	5 sets	1990

The train fleet was completely replaced with 34 brand-new Voyager (non-tilt) and 44 Super Voyager (tilting) diesel trains although four of the Super Voyagers are used by Virgin West Coast to operate services between London Euston and Holyhead.

The trains were built by Bombardier Transportation in Brugge and fitted out at that company's factory in Wakefield between 2000 and 2003. To ensure effective maintenance for a fleet which covers over one million miles a month a purpose-built depot was built by Bombardier at

a cost of £30 million at Central Rivers near Burton-on-Trent. Each train is diagrammed to return to Central Rivers twice a week.

Even with the new trains having such impressive technical specifications (see Appendix B) reports were reaching rail passenger representative groups which suggested they were not a success in the eyes of the customers using the trains. These were repeated in the media in general. The National Passenger Survey conducted by the Strategic Rail Authority in 2003 was at odds with these reports, indeed, suggesting that the opposite was in fact true.

The Authority's National Passenger Survey scores show Virgin CrossCountry had in fact made great strides between 2001 and 2004. The results are reproduced below:

National Passenger Survey: customer satisfaction scores shown in per cent:

	2001	2002	2003	2004
Overall opinion of journey	65	78	83	85
Punctuality	46	65	66	77
Frequency of trains	58	72	74	78
Comfort of seats	71	68	80	79
Cleanliness of trains	72	72	89	90
How staff handle requests	n/a	82	89	88

Some of the concerns voiced had been lack of seating capacity (especially in the four-car units), poor provision of luggage space, inadequate toilet provision and unclear seat reservation information. Concerned at the negative feedback surrounding a brand-new train fleet the Rail Passengers Committee for North Western England took the lead in conducting an independent study which would show what passengers really thought of the Voyagers. (The Regional Rail Passengers Committees had existed by statute with a remit to promote and protect the interests of rail passengers). The study involved questioning 1,030 passengers (15 per cent of whom were travelling in club class) travelling on 132 Voyager/Super Voyager trains. Five routes were surveyed:

- Birmingham–North East
- Birmingham–Reading/South Coast
- Birmingham–South West
- Birmingham–North West
- Birmingham–Manchester

Overall, some 90 per cent of passengers surveyed gave positive feedback about the Virgin experience showing that they did in fact like the new trains, thus supporting the National Passenger Survey results supplied by the Strategic Rail Authority. There were two main areas however which gave cause for concern. These were:

- Lack of luggage space (the survey showed that 43 per cent of passengers were travelling with suitcases).
- A perceived degree of overcrowding.

Virgin Trains tackled the first point by removing some seats to allow for more luggage storage, but the second reflects not only the fact that Voyagers are shorter than the trains they replaced but also the growing numbers of people wishing to travel by rail. Ultimately the only answer is additional carriages but at around £1.5 million per coach this is an expensive requirement and unlikely to be achieved during the present franchise. CrossCountry Franchise Director Brian Johnson explained that crowding is an issue on certain trains within the core sections of route, but that it only happens on about 15–20 per cent of a typical unit's day in service. This makes it very difficult to put a business case together for additional carriages and a sound business case can only be made if it is spread over the lifetime use of a carriage. Since this could be 30 plus years no individual operator can take responsibility for the full cost of this in its own right because none of the franchises have been let for that length of time. It may therefore need the Department for Transport to be co-signatories to protect the long-term investment of the ROSCO involved, which would probably need some sort of assurance that its trains would still be used or funded if network requirements changed.

Virgin Trains' vision for CrossCountry included the operation of more-frequent services to more destinations and in fact, some 115 towns and cities would be served. This required the introduction of regular clockfaced timetables using Birmingham New Street as the hub (the 'Birmingham Cross'). The plan was to use the new train fleet supported by refurbished and re-liveried shortened High Speed Trains from the old fleet. These would have consisted of five coaches and were to be known as Challengers. These were to be used on the proposed Blackpool–Paddington services via the Stroud Valley although unfortunately, the plan never came to fruition because CrossCountry was unable to finance the retention of the trains and the SRA refused to fund them. Many passengers seeing the sight of trains withdrawn from service with the Virgin franchises but still being operated by other TOCs and carrying the famous Virgin Trains livery found this difficult

Cheered on by enthusiasts, Class 47 No 47077 *North Star* **tops Lickey Incline with the last loco-hauled Virgin CrossCountry service from Penzance to Manchester Piccadilly on 19 August 2002. The public train terminated at Birmingham New Street but then went on with invited guests to Derby while a new Virgin Voyager continued the journey to Manchester.**
Virgin Trains / Milepost 92$^{1/2}$

Above: **A Virgin CrossCountry Class 47** locomotive runs light engine through the 'Potteries' as it crosses the canal at Kidsgrove.
Virgin Trains / Milepost 92^{1/2}

Right: **CrossCountry Class 47 No 47822** *Pride of Shrewsbury* arrives with a terminating train at the low level platforms of Portsmouth & Southsea.
Virgin Trains / Milepost 92^{1/2}

to accept, though the use of five-car trains on the Cheltenham–Paddington route may well have proved inadequate for the peak time services. Although the number of trains running would have increased considerably they would all have comprised fewer carriages than their predecessors. Even so, the actual number of seats on the trains overall would have seen an increase.

The change over and introduction to the new services was code named 'Operation Princess' and formed the basis of CrossCountry's business plan. This was intended to see ten services leave Birmingham every hour, five to the North and five to the South, but of course this required the ten balancing services arriving at New Street. In all, some 424 Voyager and Super Voyager movements were required every day at an already very busy station.

The 212 daily departures from Birmingham New Street include:

- 51 to North West/Scotland
- 35 to North East/Scotland
- 44 to South West
- 33 to Reading/South Coast

Included in these totals were:

Birmingham to:	No of weekday trains	Fastest journey
Reading	31	1hr 28min
Bristol	30	1hr 24min
Manchester	33	1hr 34min
Sheffield	31	1hr 09min
Leeds	17	1hr 52min

A six-point plan was devised to achieve:
1. A £1 billion investment in new trains
2. Britain's first national interval timetable
3. Journey times cut by 20 per cent
4. Double train frequencies
5. Double the number of passengers carried
6. Elimination of subsidy within ten years

A regular interval timetable had already existed on some of Britain's InterCity routes but only been on those serving London. These had never been dovetailed into a timetable which served the country as a whole, but Operation Princess included plans to do this. The obvious benefits from such a timetable would not just be ideal for

Virgin Trains but would be beneficial to other train operators too. A high degree of co-operation would be required from Railtrack (effectively the timetable custodian) and each of the other train operating companies.

Table 51 in the National Rail Timetable shows how complex the CrossCountry timetable had become. It was the result of 20 years of fine tuning and every train had to be individually pathed through a host of congested junctions resulting in very few being timetabled to a regular interval. The final timetable for Operation Princess was the result of more than three years consultation with other train operators, Railtrack, the Rail

Top: **A Class 86 electric locomotive, fresh from the paint-shop, shows off its new Virgin Trains colours at Crewe during 1999.**
Virgin Trains / Milepost 92$^{1/2}$

Above: **Evening at Crewe and Virgin Trains Class 86 No 86251** *The Birmingham Post* **is ready for departure.**
Virgin Trains / Milepost 92$^{1/2}$

Regulator, Strategic Rail Authority and other stakeholders. Although it ran to more than 80 drafts before it was ready to be introduced, the end product was a much more simplified timetable.

Operation Princess arrived amid high publicity in September 2002, and with excited youngsters dressed as princesses travelling to Birmingham New Street from the major cities served by CrossCountry and the company being closely watched by the media.

Enormous effort had been put into the production of the new timetable and certainly on paper, it was workable. The difficulty with CrossCountry's services though is clear, in that they have to run through such well known rail bottlenecks as Bristol, Manchester, Newcastle, Reading, Sheffield and the mother of them all, Birmingham. There are many others and it can only take one train to be delayed for a few min-

utes for the knock-on effect to gather momentum. Since it is impossible to run any railway without delays occurring somewhere it is not surprising that on Britain's crowded lines the new timetable began to pose performance headaches.

Realising that as it stood, Operation Princess was unsustainable, CrossCountry and its industry associates returned to the drawing board and quickly came up with a revised version. It is worth remembering though, that the revised timetable contained hardly any alterations over the core sections of most routes, but changed turn-rounds at the end of journeys to make the product deliverable. Indeed, the May 2006 timetable at Birmingham New Street reflects the original 2002 version for CrossCountry services at the station. This time it not only worked on paper but also in reality.

The timetable revisions could not by themselves solve all the performance issues at a stroke, and it was obvious to all that certain long distance trains were regularly poor performers. One solution was to take a close look at train regulation e.g. should certain trains take priority over others. Virgin Trains was not the only operator to be suffering from this and negotiations with all concerned saw a trial take place. In CrossCountry's case the obvious choice was the 1S66 service from Penzance to Dundee. This train formed part of the afternoon peak service in Scotland and was redesignated 9S66 and was to be given priority at bottlenecks wherever possible. The experiment was successful and delays to this service were considerably reduced.

Performance on other routes also improved and this, coupled with the new trains, saw a

Above: **A Virgin High Speed Train, headed by No 43086, is seen at Carlisle Citadel forming a service bound for Edinburgh on 10 April 2003.** *Peter W. Robinson*

Right: **Virgin CrossCountry HST No 43160 is reflected in the wet platform at Birmingham New Street in 2001.** *Virgin Trains / Milepost 92¹/²*

surge in the popularity of CrossCountry's services. Virgin Trains were now faced with a capacity issue since on some routes seven-car HSTs had been replaced with the shorter Voyagers. As mentioned earlier, VT would have liked to have seen an additional carriage in each of the new trains, but did not have the means of financing them. A possible answer would have been to join Voyager sets together to make trains longer and either retain some of the HSTs to cover for the Voyagers so used, or alternatively purchase additional Voyager trains. Both options were expensive and would have needed further subsidy from government, and this was not available. It is likely that the SRA would have been content for CrossCountry to have the extra trains, but only if the company could raise the funding itself. Ultimately, this proved impossible and Virgin Trains certainly could not risk raising fares to an astronomical level to finance it.

CrossCountry's business case was now being threatened because it required the combination of route upgrade, new train fleet and additional services to link together for it to work. So, despite the impressive new trains Virgins' vision to eradicate government subsidy for the CrossCountry franchise was proving impossible to achieve although impressive increases in the number of passengers being carried had been attained. Some of the causes were outside Virgin Trains' control and are examined elsewhere in this book, but by May 2005 the CrossCountry network had been reduced to 1,550 route miles and a glance at any map of Britain shows the similarity between CrossCountry's routes to that of the motorway network. However, although the number of route miles had fallen from the 1994 level, the number of passengers carried each year had almost doubled to an impressive 19 million with the then 104 trains running each day increasing to 184 today.

One of CrossCountry's HST sets crosses Brunel's Royal Albert Bridge as it enters Devon, in the summer of 2002.
Virgin Trains / Milepost 92¹ᐟ²

Top: **A CrossCountry HST crosses the River Tamar via Brunel's famous bridge at Saltash, on its way to Penzance.** *Virgin Trains / Milepost 92¹/²*

Above: **Another CrossCountry HST traverses the famous sea wall at Dawlish in Devon.** *Virgin Trains / Milepost 92¹/²*

CrossCountry's own surveys show that the average mileage for each passenger is 83 miles. The tables below indicate the average age of CrossCountry passengers and the purpose of their journeys.

Customer age profile:

Years	%
16–24	37
25–44	32
45–59	19
60+	12

(Passengers aged less than 16 years were not asked to complete the survey.)

Journey purpose:

	%
Visiting friends or relatives	41
Business	23
Shopping, other leisure or personal business	15
Holiday or short break	13
Work, school or college	8

Since the introduction of the Voyager and Super Voyager fleets in 2002, CrossCountry has witnessed a 54 per cent increase in passengers travelling for business purposes. By 2006, the core section between Birmingham and Leeds was regularly witnessing standing passengers in both First and Standard Classes reflecting this increase. Because of the growing importance of Birmingham as a business centre some long-distance services from Plymouth, Bournemouth, Preston, Leeds and Newcastle are timed to arrive in Birmingham before 10.00, with trains from Exeter, Southampton and York before 09.00. Services from Manchester are also timed to arrive in time for business meetings, thus avoiding the need for unwanted overnight stays. All the trains serve Birmingham's New Street station, which is convenient for the International Convention Centre. Additionally, many services from North West England, Exeter, Reading and Bournemouth stop at Birmingham International station which

is adjacent to the National Exhibition Centre, and also serves Birmingham International Airport.

Conversely, CrossCountry also links Birmingham (and other major towns and cities) with other conference venues such as Bournemouth, Brighton, Torquay and Glasgow as well as having convenient connections with major exhibition centres including Manchester's GMEX centre. The increase in business use on CrossCountry services has given strong support to the creation of First Class lounges at Birmingham New Street, Coventry, Stoke-on-Trent, Manchester and Wolverhampton.

There has also been an increase in leisure travellers using senior railcards to obtain discounted first class rail travel. For these passengers the provision of first class lounges is welcome. CrossCountry does not operate any stations itself despite the large number at which it calls, and the first class lounges listed above are all found at the stations of its sister company, Virgin West Coast. Despite not being a station facilities operator CrossCountry works closely with other train operating companies to ensure that assistance, facilities and information is available for its passengers. Virgin CrossCountry has its own customer service teams at Birmingham New Street and Edinburgh Waverley stations specifically for those purposes.

Despite the increasing popularity of its CrossCountry services the company's financial position had worsened and seriously threatened its future. Realising the seriousness of the situation, Virgin Trains had to return to the Strategic Rail Authority who entered into negotiations aimed at keeping trains running on both fran-

chises. Ultimately, letters of agreement were drawn up in 2004, these really being a supplement to the existing franchises. For CrossCountry time was becoming crucial. The franchise urgently needed its finances supporting and whilst the SRA would probably have preferred a longer time span to resolve the situation, CrossCountry was in a position whereby it had to insist on a deadline for the letter of agreement to be signed.

An interview with Virgin Trains Chief Executive, Tony Collins, revealed just how serious the situation had become. Virgin Rail Group always knew that it would take until at least 2008/09 for the CrossCountry franchise to move from receiving government subsidy to becoming a premium payer. On the other hand, its sister franchise at

Top: **An HST forming part of Edinburgh's commuter service is seen crossing the Forth Bridge in 2001.**
Virgin Trains / Milepost 92$^{1/2}$

Above: **A VT CrossCountry High Speed Train passes Southampton Airport Parkway with a service from Bournemouth.**
Virgin Trains / Milepost 92$^{1/2}$

Right: A Virgin Trains HST speeds south from Crewe, Cheshire under a heavy array of overhead line equipment.
Virgin Trains / Milepost 92$^{1/2}$

Below: A Virgin CrossCountry HST passes an old Cornish tin mine near Redruth with the UK's longest daily main line run from Aberdeen to Penzance, in 2002.
Virgin Trains / Milepost 92$^{1/2}$

Bottom: A High Speed Train on a Virgin CrossCountry service takes a well-earned breather at Totnes in Devon.
Virgin Trains / Milepost 92$^{1/2}$

West Coast expected to reach a premium paying situation much more quickly. The plan was that during the transition of CrossCountry it would receive support from West Coast. The demise of Railtrack and cutbacks on the West Coast Route Modernisation meant that West Coast itself would take longer to reach premium payer status. Consequently it would not be able to give the intended support to its sister company as had been planned.

The letters of agreement for the two franchises did differ in one major way. The Strategic Rail Authority wanted the CrossCountry letter of agreement to include a 'no fault termination' clause, which West Coast's did not. That reflected the stronger financial position of the West Coast franchise. CrossCountry agreed to the clause being inserted in order to reach a conclusion to the negotiations. So serious was the situation that Tony Collins told the author that Virgin Trains was within one hour of having to walk away from the franchises. Fortunately, the agreements were signed and passengers are now receiving the benefits of improved performance on both CrossCountry and West Coast routes.

The final bid from CrossCountry to resume normal operation of the franchise had been considered to be too expensive and the 'no fault termination' clause was invoked by the SRA to end the franchise early. This effectively meant Virgin Trains now ran services on behalf of the SRA with the Authority supplying the funding. It also protected Virgin Trains from suffering what would have been unsustainable costs and CrossCountry would receive a fee for delivering the service. CrossCountry considered itself somewhat hard done by with this decision because many of the costs involved related to the track access charges made by Network Rail and would still be payable whoever held the franchise. The decision also came at a time when CrossCountry was seeing

Above: **An Anglo-Scottish CrossCountry HST pauses at a wintry Stockport in 2001.**
Virgin Trains / Milepost 92$^{1/2}$

Left: **Passengers in a Virgin hot air balloon enjoy a grandstand view as one of Virgin CrossCountry's HSTs tops the Lickey Incline, heading north in 2001.**
Virgin Trains / Milepost 92$^{1/2}$

huge increases in performance, reliability and customer satisfaction. Rumours were rife that CrossCountry would be split up and the services transferred to other train operating companies. An attempt to do this had been made before privatisation, but the complex nature of the operation made it impossible to do so.

It is now known that the CrossCountry route map will change significantly towards the end of 2007, when the number of franchisees is reduced and further routes will fall into a revised CrossCountry network. The changes will result in the CrossCountry franchise no longer serving Brighton or stations along the West Coast Main Line north of Crewe and Manchester (some of these services will be trans-ferred to Virgin West Coast), with Edinburgh services travelling via the East Coast route. Additionally though, it will be required to serve Cardiff, Nottingham, Stansted Airport and provide the local Birmingham–Leicester services.

The author suspects that the desire to see a reduction in the overall number of franchisees was a significant factor in the decision to end the CrossCountry franchise early. As part of the reorganisation the CrossCountry franchise will be re-let from November 2007 for a period of 8 years 4 months, and the newly formed Virgin Voyager Trains Ltd has submitted a bid on behalf of the Virgin Rail Group for the New Cross Country franchise in November 2006.

Behind the Scenes
(Cross Country Trains Ltd)

Just as we had a look behind the scenes at West Coast earlier, we shall now do the same with CrossCountry and find out just how difficult it was in practice to bring the new trains into revenue-earning service. Again, an in depth interview with Chris Green provided candid answers revealing details that were never in the public eye and showing how, whenever one problem was overcome another stepped in to replace it.

Voyagers and Super Voyagers

The non-tilting Voyagers were deliberately built first in 2000 to get testing experience, and the tilting Super Voyagers followed in 2002. The Voyagers were built at Bombardier's core plant in Brugge, Belgium which was Bombardier's engineering power base in Europe and offered a well-managed and busy production line.

Bombardier won the contract to deliver an inter-city diesel-electric multiple unit (DEMU) that could operate at 125mph using underfloor diesel engines driving electric motors. This design had the huge advantage that the electric motors could simply be turned into invertors (i.e. in reverse), to decelerate the train down to 20mph. This rheostatic braking has proved highly successful and has brought high braking performance with minimum wear and tear.

The Voyagers were built to time and budget and the first unit, No 220001 *Maiden Voyager*,

A Virgin Voyager carriage under construction at Bombardier's Wakefield factory in 2001.
Virgin Trains / Milepost 92½

was handed over to Sir Richard Branson and Brian Souter at a major public relations event at Brugge on 6 December 2000. The guests had the unusual treat of travelling on a test run on Belgian National Railways (SNCB) to Ostend and back, the Voyager working straight 'out of the box'.

The Belgium run was possible because Bombardier had submitted the Voyager for an SNCB safety case, which took just nine days compared to the year or more that was becoming normal under UK bureaucracy. The Belgian driver on the day declared the train to have the best braking system he had ever driven, and he must have been on to something because it was subsequently toned down a little after traffic experience in the UK.

The Voyagers began to stream across to the UK, and reached a steady rate of one or more sets delivered every week throughout 2001. They were given their UK test run at Crofton, outside Wakefield, before being handed over for traffic. A small number of specialist Virgin Trains drivers had been allocated to Crofton for the test runs and they became an elite band that raced up and down the East Coast route at 125mph to ensure that all the systems were fully operational. They rarely found much wrong and a day over the pit was usually enough to see the trains signed off.

The end of the old fleet

Whilst the introduction of the new Voyagers and Super Voyagers went well for a brand-new fleet, the old fleet was hit with every bit of bad luck that could be imagined in its final two years. Chris Tibbitts, as Director of Operations at Birmingham, was faced with an endless sequence of unwanted challenges.

The first problem was the condition of the equipment. The Class 47 and 86 locomotives and their Mk 2 coaches were more than 30 years old and well past their 'sell by date'. The High Speed Trains were being run into the ground on stop-start services that they were never designed to undertake. British Rail InterCity had spotted all this in 1990 when it started urgent work on a replacement case for the CrossCountry fleet, based on cascaded West Coast Mk 3 sets working push-pull with new or refurbished diesel locomotives. Whitehall, though, refused to discuss any investment in replacement fleets, preferring to wait for privatisation.

The price of this near ten-year delay came home to roost from 2000 onwards. Virgin Trains found itself owning a pensionable CrossCountry fleet that needed intensive care and attention from a home depot. In fact, the opposite happened. Bombardier had been persuaded to take the old fleets into their new maintenance contract, along with the Voyagers. In hindsight, this proved a mistake, as their expertise and commitment lay with the new Voyager fleet. They just did not have the knowledge or affinity to give the older fleet the tender loving care it needed. Bombardier found itself making contracts with around 14 depots owned by rival train companies, which might have gone that extra mile to support old colleagues in the CrossCountry team, but who had no rapport with Bombardier.

The result was a deterioration in fleet reliability and quality which was to be accelerated by a series of crises. The first was the now long-forgotten floods of autumn 2000 across the UK which created a serious safety problem for the old Mk 2 fleet when they ran through deep water. This led to severe wheel damage as the water caused the steel tyres to loosen and at one stage, half the fleet was withdrawn and three-coach trains were being run.

The second was the Hatfield accident in October 2000, which led to endless 20mph speed restrictions across the UK. This hit CrossCountry especially badly because it travelled over a high percentage of the restrictions and both the timetable and the maintenance regimes were decimated.

The third was the hot summer of 2002 which played havoc with the poorly maintained HST fleet, causing engines to overheat. Space and priority was becoming a problem at the major maintenance depots as the arriving Voyager fleet was jostling for attention with the older trains.

Top: **Compare the previous photograph with this interior view of a completed standard class carriage of a Virgin Voyager.** *Michael Hughes*

Above: **A driving motor car for a Voyager unit under construction at Bombardier's Wakefield factory in 2002. The crash protection area is clearly visible.**
Virgin Trains / Milepost 92$^{1/2}$

Left: **A Virgin Voyager minus its under gear during construction at Bombardier's Wakefield works in 2002.**
Peter W. Robinson

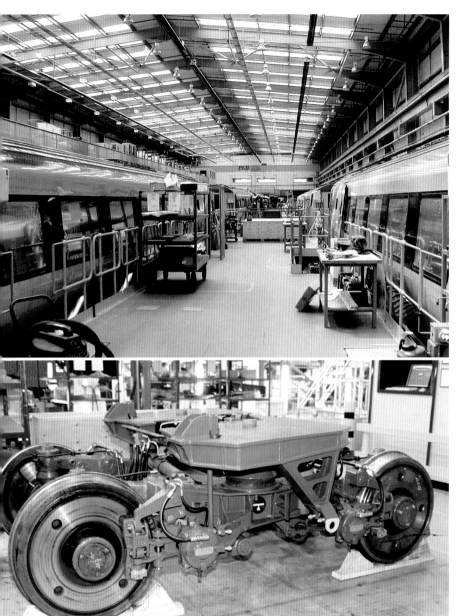

By 2002, as much management effort was going into maintaining the old fleet in its last gasp as was going into commissioning the new trains. This was probably partially the result of Virgin's decision not to employ the maintenance staff it inherited with the franchises. VT had to strengthen its management resources for the old fleet and 'Mac' McIntosh – who went on to make a success of the South West Trains fleet maintenance – was brought in to keep the HSTs running to the end. He remembers this as one of his toughest and least glamorous jobs.

In summary, the CrossCountry fleet should have been renewed or refurbished ten years previously in 1990, as InterCity had planned. The additional ten years delay gave Virgin Trains an impossible task which put an intolerable burden on managers and resulted in a deteriorating service which lost both reputation and passenger confidence.

Beginning of the new fleet

The Voyagers were a largely trouble-free train which had been well designed for ease of maintenance. They were the first fleet to feature the new inside frame bogies which had been developed by British Rail at the Derby Research Centre.

The train maintenance arrangements were not so trouble free, however. The original Virgin Trains/Bombardier concept was for a train that ran virtually maintenance free for three days and then reported to a central service depot for overnight examination. This proved to be a rather naïve assumption for a fleet of trains that was to be worked twice as hard as the old ones and which would be spread across the UK every night at 14 outbases spread between Aberdeen and Penzance.

The plan was for the outbases to fuel and clean the trains, and service the toilets, leaving the Central Rivers 'mother ship' to undertake maintenance and repairs. Back on planet Earth, life was rather different. Trains were arriving at remote

Top: **Voyagers and Super Voyagers are seen under construction at Bombardier in 2002.**
Peter W. Robinson

Above: **One of the newly designed inside-frame Voyager bogies awaits fitting at Bombardier. The small wheels of these trains can clearly be seen.**
Virgin Trains / Milepost 92¹/²

Right: **A Voyager body shell arrives by road transport for fitting out at the Wakefield works of Bombardier in 2001.**
Virgin Trains / Milepost 92¹/²

service points at the end of the day with engines isolated, windscreens smashed by vandals, and doors out of use. There were other issues too although this was not the fault of the train, more it was real life, in probably the harshest railway operating environment in the UK. Most other inter-city fleets stay on one line of route and return to a major depot owned by their company every night. CrossCountry trains typically run up to 3,000 miles for three days as they criss-cross the country before they return to Central Rivers on the third day. Chris Green recollects the early meetings as Bombardier came to terms with the realities of intensive fleet operations in the punishing UK environment. As he says: 'to their eternal credit, the senior team at Bombardier took the financial hit and increased their maintenance costs substantially.' They were to be rewarded for

Top: **A Super Voyager tilt testing in southern France crosses a viaduct between Brive and Cahors in January 2002.**
Virgin Trains / Milepost 92$^{1/2}$

Above: **Sir Richard Branson and Brian Souter introduce the Virgin Voyager to the press and invited guests on 6 December 2001.**
Virgin Trains / Milepost 92$^{1/2}$

Left: **A pair of Voyagers undergoing routine maintenance at Central Rivers depot on 22 January 2004.** *Peter W. Robinson*

Above: **A trio of Voyagers displaying 'Not To Be Moved' boards while they receive attention at Central Rivers depot in 2004.**
Virgin Trains / Milepost 92¹/²

Right: **A Virgin Voyager stands outside Bombardier's Central Rivers servicing facility in August 2001.**
Virgin Trains / Milepost 92¹/²

Below right: **A four-car Voyager unit enters Central Rivers Depot for routine maintenance in 2005.**
Virgin Trains / Milepost 92¹/²

this far-sighted decision by a high-performing train that attracted further orders, first from Midland Mainline for the 'Meridians', and then by Hull Trains for their 'Pioneers'.

Central Rivers depot

The decision to build a new depot for the CrossCountry fleet was visionary and today Central Rivers is arguably one of the most modern and professional maintenance depots in the country, yet it did not even exist in 1999 when the trains were ordered. CrossCountry had evolved from the main InterCity routes, with their regional ownership and the radial mainlines to London. It effectively became a 'cuckoo in the nest' of these well-established routes and simply split its maintenance between depots such as Plymouth Laira, Edinburgh Craigentinny, Leeds Neville Hill and Manchester Longsight.

The snag was that human nature meant that even the most altruistic depot engineer was always going to give his local fleet priority over CrossCountry when a crisis arose. You only had to compare the HSTs maintained by East Coast or Great Western with the similar HSTs they looked after for CrossCountry to realise that the Voyagers just had to have a dedicated depot of their own if they were to become a quality fleet.

Bombardier had won a £600 million maintenance contract to 2012 when they secured the construction contract and they totally accepted that quality maintenance meant buying 'Cinderella' a house at last. They committed to build a brand-new, £30 million depot on a greenfield site at Central Rivers, near Burton-on-Trent. The site is superbly located close to the heart of the CrossCountry operations at Birmingham New Street. The depot was built with access at both ends and is so large that it can hold a third of the fleet overnight for maintenance and cleaning.

Central Rivers has had its struggles, but it has now settled down as a centre of excellence for train engineering and is now much visited by overseas engineers. It offers the advantage of bringing the entire engineering, design, stores and planning fleet expertise into one place. It is able to offer skilled advice to the major outbases and will frequently send an overnight trouble-shooting team in a well-equipped van to get a train back into service quickly.

Super Voyagers

The Super Voyager fleet was more complex and was therefore always going to be more troublesome than the Voyager. These are 44 tilting trains which were bought to deliver 125mph speeds over the more curvaceous West Coast route, in partnership with their electric Pendolino cousins. However, whereas the Pendolino was conceived as a tilting train from the beginning, and the UK was the ninth country to purchase the Fiat design, the Super Voyager was conceived as a non-tilting train and had to be so adapted. The result has been a train where every coach weighs five tonnes more than the Voyager for the same 750hp per vehicle. Moreover, the tilt is limited to six degrees compared to the eight degrees of the Pendolino. This prevents the Super Voyager from cornering as fast as its cousin and has led to dual speed boards on some curves.

The best decision on the Super Voyagers was the commitment to build virtually the entire sub fleet as five-car units. This was done to meet the expected growth in passenger numbers. The four-car Voyagers have now become embarrassingly overcrowded due to an almost doubling of passengers travelling on the CrossCountry network, although such has been the growth that even the Super Voyagers are now seeing the same problem.

The approach to the Central Rivers depot with two Voyagers standing on the refuelling lines.
Virgin Trains / Milepost 92$^{1/2}$

ered as a family style. He also wanted to get the Voyager name into people's vocabulary.

Around the beginning of the 1970s many of the UK's branch lines were closed, falling victim to the axe being wielded by the government of the day. Today we are fortunate that some have been re-opened as heritage lines by preservationist groups and members of the Voyager family have visited such lines, where they could be seen alongside restored steam engines from yesteryear. One such line was the route from Wareham to Swanage, which closed in January 1972. The Swanage Railway, working in conjunction with Virgin Trains, Railtrack and Balfour Beatty, was able to restore the connection to the main line at Wareham, and 8 September 2002 saw the first through working for over 30 years. The brand new £4million Voyager No 220018 worked through to Swanage where it was named *Dorset Voyager* by Moyra Cross and Stan Symes of the Swanage Railway.

Swanage was not the only preserved line to see visits from Virgin's Voyagers. The North Yorkshire Moors Railway, Severn Valley Railway and West Somerset Railway all being treated to the sight of the latest trains on their metals.

Green saw the Voyagers and Super Voyagers as two related families and felt that the differentiation would also help operating staff at the workface. The 34 Voyagers were given red nameplates with geographical names such as *Black Country Voyager, Grampian Voyager* and *Solent Voyager* etc. The 44 Super Voyagers were given blue nameplates and named after famous actual voyagers such as Sir Walter Raleigh, Scott of the Antarctic and not forgetting Dr Who!

125mph track Birmingham–Sheffield

Today, we take for granted the modern high-speed track between Birmingham and Sheffield that allows the Voyager family of trains to run at up to 125mph without tilt, but it nearly didn't happen. The original aspiration was to get 125mph running from Taunton to York, with the obvious exceptions through Bristol and West Yorkshire. This would then have joined up with the 125mph running on the East Coast and West Coast main lines.

An investment case was quickly made for the Birmingham to Sheffield section, but upgrading the remaining stretch between Birmingham and Taunton could not be justified because of the costly upgrading of level crossings and signalling. The decision was taken to divide the upgrading into two stages and push ahead with the first without delay, and as Chris Green said: 'a bird in the hand was better than no bird.' He still remains extremely disappointed that the section paralleling the M5 motorway remains a 90mph railway.

Even so, the Birmingham to Sheffield section upgrade nearly did not happen. The £200 million investment scheme depended upon a complex

Top: **A CrossCountry Voyager waits at Reading's platform 7 before forming the 13:48 service to Bournemouth in 2004.** *John Balmforth*

Above: **A Super Voyager waits to depart York with a service to Birmingham New Street on 17 June 2004.** *Michael Hughes*

The Super Voyagers were given a spectacular test site in the French Dordogne area, where they tilted daily at high speeds between Brive-la-Gaillarde and Limoges to get mileage experience. On the last day, Chris Green travelled across with the railway trade press to re-name No 221101 *Louis Bleriot,* and unveiled the first blue-backed Super Voyager nameplate.

Voyager and Super Voyager namings

The decision was taken in 1999 to name the entire Voyager and Pendolino fleets by the time the last units were delivered. Chris Green was influenced by the old Class 52 *'Western'* diesel-hydraulic fleet which had been named and deliv-

A sizeable crowd boarding a CrossCountry Voyager bound for Plymouth at York on 17 June 2004. One of the benefits of CrossCountry services is the opportunity to make long-distance journeys without having to change trains. *Michael Hughes*

legal contract in which Railtrack agreed to bring some track renewals forward with Virgin Trains paying part of the enhancement cost of increasing the line speed from 90mph to 125mph through increased access charges. The timing could not have been worse, because with Railtrack in Railway Administration a linespeed improvement was never going to be a high priority investment for a High Court administrator.

Creditably though, Railtrack stood by the scheme and honoured its commitment to Virgin Trains and to the local communities. The new Chief Executive, Steve Marshall, personally championed the scheme and signed the deal with Chris Green (on behalf of Virgin Trains) at the height of the problems. The upgrade then became a Railtrack project in the teeth of the Hatfield re-railing crisis. Chris Green remembers endless progress-chasing to ensure that the upgrade had its fair share of weekend engineering possessions and new track. Despite valiant efforts, the work was only partly finished for the new CrossCountry timetable in September 2002 and was to cost the Voyagers three vital extra minutes in the accelerated timetable which should have been used to improve performance. Project management was so chaotic in that period that it was to be Easter 2006 before the final section was relaid in Clay Cross Tunnel and all speed restrictions removed.

The new timetable

Gigantic efforts went into a total rewrite of the CrossCountry timetable for September 2002. Chris Green always recognised that this was going to be a high-risk event, because the entire CrossCountry timetable had to be changed on the same day across much of the UK.

The new timetable was so radical that it virtu-

ally doubled the number of CrossCountry trains through Birmingham New Street at a stroke. Nine trains of the Voyager family were to arrive every hour and nine were to depart – usually the same trains continuing journeys across Birmingham. This pattern would be repeated every hour in a radical break from the rather ragged old CrossCountry timetable. In addition, there would be a number of empty stock or positioning movements.

The train services were not only just about to double, they were also going to get faster. The Voyagers and Super Voyagers could outpace just about every train on the tracks when they were first introduced, and this meant that many other operators' routes had to have their timetables redrafted on the same day to match the new slots and maintain connections.

Then there was the consultation. Two years were spent with *'in detailed'* consultations across the country with fellow train operators, Passenger Transport Executives (PTEs), local government, regional Rail Passengers Committees and other stakeholders. The resulting timetable reached its 80th draft before an acceptable compromise was reached. The final timetable then had to be presented to the Rail Regulator in a formal hearing where still further objections and changes arose.

The final timetable was then given to Railtrack in November 2001, just ten months before the 'drop-dead' date for the public timetable in September 2002. Even so, this was *not* the timetable – at that stage it was only the commercial 'wish list' underwritten by the Rail Regulator. Railtrack's train planners now had to turn it into slots that worked, and without upsetting the rights of around 30 other train operators.

With hindsight, this was probably mission-

impossible for the newly privatised rail industry. There was effectively no central timetable direction, although six regional timetabling offices did their best to help. Again, Chris Green remembers sitting through a procession of increasingly desperate meetings as the planners tried every which way to juggle their overcrowded railways.

The net result was a timetable that was to prove too tight to work, but there was no overall operations department to take the lead on the delivery problems. Yes, CrossCountry had got its two hourly services through to destinations such as Liverpool, Cardiff and Portsmouth, but the paths were so tight, with the turn rounds lacking suffi-cient time, that trains regularly ran late and had to be turned back before reaching their destinations.

When CrossCountry had won the franchise in 1997 there was probably room on the tracks for most of its proposals, but the welcome decision to buy new trains brought a penalty of waiting five years before the new timetable could be introduced. In that time other train operating companies had been adding their own new services and obtaining access rights. A good example of this is the Birmingham–Derby corridor which originally had one fast train and one stopping train per hour. Central Trains first added one train then the Operation Princess timetable put forward by CrossCountry added a second fast train making four in all. However, Central Trains held access rights to introduce a further stopping service which it did, running from Matlock to Birmingham. Turn round times were so short that on a busy route late running was inevitable, with both CrossCountry and Central Trains services suffering delays. Neither operator had done anything wrong but better planning on Railtrack's part might have been beneficial to all concerned.

There is also, little doubt that some companies learnt of the CrossCountry proposals from the public consultation meetings and then inserted their own services ahead of the game to ensure that they increased their share of the ORCATS income allocations. (ORCATS is the mechanism by which revenue is shared between operators where more than one company operates over the same or part routes.)

In looking back at the sorry tale it is obvious that Railtrack was a major player in the failure of the full Operation Princess timetable. CrossCountry held track access rights from the

beginning of its franchise (and still does), which enabled it to legally introduce the additional services including those along the Stroud Valley into Paddington, which never came to fruition. The trouble was that other train operators also held rights to introduce their new services. The central problem in Tony Collins' words was: 'incompetence on the part of Railtrack' because it did not realise it had oversold capacity.

Cinderella to Princess

The new CrossCountry timetable launch had been code named Operation Princess to symbolise the huge changes that were about to arrive. CrossCountry had always been the poor relation – it was superimposed on the old regions – and received few new trains and never had a dedicated engineering depot of its own. Its services did not operate at regular intervals and were generally slower than routes serving London.

Now, CrossCountry was to see its entire fleet renewed in just two years, its train frequency doubled, its services making regular interval calls and its journey times accelerated. It really was Cinderella to Princess and it was worth celebrating. Both staff and public morale were high in anticipation of a £1 billion investment in CrossCountry.

Virgin Trains' Julie Beck-Richards helped organise a very successful corporate affairs programme which involved the entire community in the forthcoming launch. Voyagers and Super Voyagers visited every part of the CrossCountry empire for high speed demonstration runs and naming ceremonies. On launch day itself, Sir Richard Branson positioned himself at Birmingham as special parties arrived from all

points of the compass. Regional television gave the new service a warm welcome throughout the country and 78 children dressed as princesses and representing the 78 trains and their towns paraded for the cameras.

Within a week though, it was clear that the new timetable was not going to deliver the goods. There were two basic problems; the train slots were just too tight to deliver reliably – many line speed schemes were late – and there was excessive overcrowding on some trains. It normally takes at least a year to change a timetable and now the challenge was to make radical changes within weeks. To everyone's credit the temptation to hold a witch hunt was avoided and the same teams worked together to create a 'plan B' as rapidly as possible. The instinct for

Top: **A Voyager and a Super Voyager coupled together make a wonderful sight as they cross Ribblehead Viaduct on 26 March 2005.** *Peter W. Robinson*

Above: **Youngsters dressed as princesses congregate in Birmingham as part of the celebrations heralding the arrival of 'Operation Princess'. They had travelled from most of the major cities on the CrossCountry network.** *Virgin Trains / Milepost 92$^{1/2}$*

apportioning blame was avoided by all parties and Chris Green accepted responsibility and ensured that there would be no incriminations.

He attended all the meetings both to hear about the problems and to help fast-tracking the solutions. The experts quickly identified the worst bottlenecks and the most overcrowded trains and a series of action plans was triggered to slacken train schedules, lengthen the most overcrowded trains, increase the luggage space on Voyagers and hand some routes over to other operators who could offer additional rolling stock.

Chris Green feels that good came out of the whole CrossCountry timetable episode as well as evil. An immature private industry realised that it had to work together at times to deliver major timetable improvements. From that point onwards co-operation was the name of the game, and the Strategic Rail Authority provided the missing central leadership for the industry. Chris also points out that the innocent players in the game were the Voyager and Super Voyager fleets themselves saying: 'It is a compliment to the engineers that the new trains performed well throughout those difficult opening weeks and were certainly not the cause of CrossCountry's problems.'

CrossCountry – a new managing director

One of the biggest realisations was that CrossCountry and West Coast were too big to be run as a single Virgin Trains operation and from 2003 they were effectively run as two independent train operating companies. This was the point at which CrossCountry was given its own managing director for the first time, this being Chris Gibb who arrived from Wales & Borders and he restored the tight management focus that CrossCountry had enjoyed in its British Rail days

Top: **A double Voyager set departs Banbury on 10 April 2004 with a northbound CrossCountry service.** *Peter W. Robinson*

Above: **Two Virgin Voyagers pass at Yarnton Lane, Kidlington.** *Virgin Trains / Milepost 92$^{1/2}$*

Right: **A CrossCountry Voyager heading for Newcastle encounters a plentiful supply of waiting passengers as it arrives at Birmingham New Street on 5 December 2002.** *Peter W. Robinson*

Above: **A southbound Virgin CrossCountry service heads for Brighton as a Virgin Atlantic Boeing 747 (G-VROM) lands at Gatwick Airport.** *Virgin Trains / Milepost 92$^{1/2}$*

Left: **Super Voyager No 221143 makes a stark contrast to the replica broad-gauge steam locomotive** *Iron Duke* **at the National Rail Museum, York on 7 October 2002.** *Virgin Trains / Milepost 92$^{1/2}$*

Right: **Virgin Trains galore as passengers board a double Voyager set at Preston.** *Virgin Trains / Milepost 92¹/₂*

Below: **Sunbathers enjoy the warm sunshine as a nine-car CrossCountry Super Voyager+Voyager service traverses the sea wall at Dawlish with a summer Saturday service for holidaymakers in July 2004.** *Virgin Trains / Milepost 92¹/₂*

under Chris Tibbits. CrossCountry is the most complex and diverse train company in Britain and needs the tight, professional focus that the new team has been able to bring.

Voyager and Super Voyager faults

This team has had its difficulties and despite the Voyagers and Super Voyagers being considered to be generally trouble free there have been problems with brake modifications, tilt commissioning and more surprisingly, with the Cummins engines overhauled by the manufacturer itself. The latter in particular, caused service disruption as trains had to be taken out of service while the problems were rectified. Dripping oil was identified as a serious problem which had resulted in some minor fires. Thankfully, this is an issue which the engineers have been able to remedy quickly.

CrossCountry suffered bad publicity when some of the new trains failed on the sea wall at Dawlish during extremely stormy conditions. The on-board computers are designed to identify faults which may damage the train and are able to shut the train down safely when such incidents occur. The heavy seas at Dawlish had given the trains involved a severe soaking and salt water ingress to component parts was resulting in the trains' systems being shut down. Normally a rebooting of the computer system will rectify the problem but in these instances, as soon as the train was restarted the safety system intervened and once again shut the engines down. Again, a simple remedy was found by engineers. An incident of a bird getting into the roof-mounted equipment caused a similar result at Penkridge.

In each of these instances passengers were delayed for several hours before being evacuated from the trains. As a result, VT held its own investigations and has now implemented a new procedure which is set in motion whenever a train fails in passenger service. This progresses through various stages, but is aimed at ensuring that passenger delays are kept to the absolute minimum.

Above: **A Virgin Voyager crosses the River Tamar into Cornwall on Brunel's Royal Albert Bridge, with a Dundee to Penzance service in 2003.** *Virgin Trains / Milepost 92¹ᐟ²*

Left: **The throat of Glasgow Central station looking south in July 2004, with commuter services and a CrossCountry Voyager in view.** *Virgin Trains / Milepost 92¹ᐟ²*

Below: **Four Voyager units coupled together hurtle under the wires on a test run along the East Coast Main Line near York in 2002.** *Virgin Trains / Milepost 92¹ᐟ²*

Above: **A double Voyager set speeds south through the beautiful Lune Gorge near Tebay in 2002.**
Virgin Trains / Milepost 92¹/²

Left: **A CrossCountry Voyager heads away from Manchester Piccadilly towards Manchester Oxford Road on its way to Scotland in 2003.**
Virgin Trains / Milepost 92¹/²

Below left: **A double CrossCountry Voyager set traverses Smardale Viaduct on the Settle & Carlisle line with a diverted service.**
Virgin Trains / Milepost 92¹/²

The effect of Hatfield on Virgin Trains

The fatal rail accident at Hatfield on 17 October 2000, coming so soon after another fatal accident at Ladbroke Grove just twelve months earlier, although not involving Virgin Trains, was to have a far-reaching effect on the two Virgin franchises and indeed, on the rail industry as a whole. The tragic facts are that a Great North Eastern Railways (GNER) express en-route from London to Leeds carrying more than 200 passengers was derailed by a broken rail while travelling at 115mph near Hatfield. The accident resulted in the tragic loss of four lives with in excess of 100 injured. It was the latest in a series of fatal rail accidents and eventually the cost, both human and financial, would play its part in the demise of Railtrack.

The immediate aftermath of the Hatfield accident saw Railtrack impose hundreds of temporary speed restrictions (TSRs) across the network while engineers checked for further track defects elsewhere. It was to be several months before all the speed restrictions were lifted and normal running resumed.

Virgin Trains, like most operators, had to implement emergency timetables since it was impossible to maintain a normal service during this period. Journey times lengthened, passenger confidence dipped and the financial consequences were enormous. Even though Virgin West Coast was not actually involved in the accident some of the financial problems it faced could be directly linked to Hatfield. The West Coast Main Line infrastructure was so poor that it was a considerable time before the TSRs along the route were removed, with the consequent loss in revenue being considerable. The business plan for West Coast in particular appeared to be in tatters, although this was also linked with the vastly increased track access charges being levied on Virgin Trains by Railtrack's successor, Network Rail, as anything else. Virgin Trains might have been able to claim compensation but this would not have been anywhere near the amount the company would have earned from the original PUG 2 upgrade. Nevertheless, some agonising decisions had to be made and Virgin West Coast chose to take a strategic view. It was a sensible decision because really, there were only a limited range of options open to them – and not all of them in any way realistic.

These included:

- Sue for the full potential loss of income.

- Pay for the upgrade itself, but a TOC on a short franchise would not be able to recoup its investment.

- Walk away from the railway altogether, but this might also have caused difficulties for its franchise partner Stagecoach.

- Work closely with Network Rail and the Strategic Rail Authority to obtain the best possible outcome for industry and passengers alike.

By choosing the wider strategic fourth possibility the outcome eventually resulted in the Pendolino trains making significant cuts in journey times between London, the North West of England and Scotland.

Virgin Trains Super Voyager driver-training simulator cab seen at Crewe Training Centre in July 2004.
John Balmforth

Staff training

On Thursday, 18 December 1998 the Associated Society of Locomotive Engineers & Firemen (ASLEF), the train drivers trade union, and Virgin Rail Group, announced an unprecedented joint training venture. Together, they formed a new company called Millennium Drivers Ltd, a fifty-fifty venture between Virgin Trains and the union, the aim of which was to become the industry leader in driver recruitment and training, promoting consistency of standards across the expanding rail network. The new company achieved a high degree of success but Virgin Trains decided to resume sole responsibility for training their own drivers around the year 2000, which resulted in the two Virgin franchises developing a state-of-the-art driver training centre at Crewe.

Following the rail accidents at Hatfield, Southall and Ladbroke Grove, the role and importance of driver training could not have had a higher profile in the eyes of both the public and the railway industry. Virgin Trains' aim of a world-class railway meant recognising this and the company spent £10 million on the new Crewe facility. That investment delivered a modern training environment and combined with the latest in simulator technology allows trainers to quite literally bring the railway into the classroom.

This meant that as of the year 2000, Virgin Trains had three full-scale cab simulators representing Class 220 Voyagers, Class 221 Super Voyagers and Class 390 Pendolinos. These were developed and managed by the French company Corys TESS. They were used to retrain all of Virgin's existing drivers on the new fleets of trains (500 CrossCountry and 450 West Coast). They are also used to test existing drivers on their safety performance during emergency and out-of-course situations whilst new drivers learn application of rules, regulations and basic driving techniques. The use of the simulators also results in impartial competence assessments, by providing an assessor and driver with a performance report generated by the simulator itself.

Every potential driver has to pass through a rigorous selection process prior to appointment. Most new drivers are from outside the railway industry, with just a small number from within, perhaps having worked as a train manager, onboard or at stations. Once accepted, trainees undergo training which Virgin Trains named its 'World Class Training Programme'. This consists

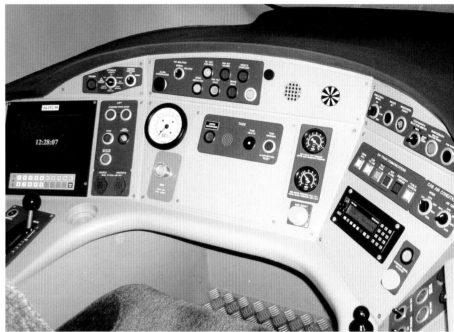

Above: **The driver's cab layout of the Virgin Trains Pendolino driver-training simulator at Crewe.** *John Balmforth*

Left: **The driver's train system status computer screen in the cab of a Pendolino.** *John Balmforth*

of over 150 days of theory and practical training, including low speed shunting in yards, a minimum of 225 hours of main line driving under supervision, use of full-task driving simulators, and low-adhesion training. On completion of the training course drivers are required to obtain in-depth knowledge of the routes over which they will be driving trains. Even then, they are required to pass a detailed route competency exam before being allowed to drive a train unsupervised.

Virgin Trains also has its own dedicated training schools at Crewe for train managers and onboard catering teams. These provide both classroom-based and 'live' practical training. It may seem a simple task to pour a cup of coffee, but on a train moving at 125mph it is a very

The author's daughter Jenny, one of the growing number of female train drivers, awaits departure at Birmingham New Street at the controls of a Voyager unit *en route* to Penzance on 5 April 2006.
John Balmforth

important skill to master. Passengers do not like hot, scalding coffee or tea in their laps. Skills in food hygiene and people management are also taught, and candidates must achieve high standards.

The train manager courses last approximately ten weeks and trainees are required to reach competency in rules, regulations, signalling, remedying technical faults with trains, first aid, safety matters, coupling and uncoupling as well as commercial training (tickets, route validity and timetables etc). As with drivers the selection process is rigorous with only the best candidates being appointed.

Station staff undergo a mixture of classroom and station-based training and are required to reach competency in rules and regulations, communication and inter-personal skills. Many are multi-skilled and competent in train despatch, ticketing, timetabling and a host of other factors including assisting passengers who have mobility difficulties. This can range from a person in a wheelchair, a mother with a pushchair and children, people with luggage or simply someone who feels vulnerable. Above all they are taught to be observant at all times. By 2003, the training teams were facilitating or presenting 850 courses and workshops each year. Whatever their level of appointment, all staff are regularly retested on their skills and competencies.

It was confirmed by Charles Belcher that every staff vacancy advertised by Virgin Trains receives large numbers of applicants and this was echoed by Brian Johnson, Franchise Director at CrossCountry, who told the author that the high number of applicants allowed the company 'to raise the bar' in its selection procedures. The author spoke to staff at all levels, from people working at stations right up to the Chairman and Chief Executive. One thing came through consistently: staff like working for Virgin Trains. I asked Chris Green (then the chair of Virgin Rail Group) what it was like working for Virgin Trains. His reply echoed that from more junior staff in that it was enjoyable. He told me that even when experiencing the many difficulties during the major upgrade works he never once received any hint of criticism or admonition from Sir Richard Branson: every phone call was supportive and uplifting. Green knew his job and Branson encouraged him to get on with it. Regular reports, yes, but no interference.

An even more forthright answer came from Virgin West Coast's Managing Director Charles Belcher. When asked by the author why he had chosen to join Virgin Trains he responded instantly with: 'because they are the biggest and the best TOC.' That attitude runs right down to the newest, most junior member of staff and is a major reason why so many applications are received for every vacancy.

Top right: **Driving cab controls of Virgin West Coast Class 57 'Thunderbird' No 57312** *The Hood*. *John Balmforth*

Above right: **The driver's view approaching London Euston on 15 March 2006.** *John Balmforth*

Left: **The driver's view approaching Reading on a wet 13 October 2004.** *John Balmforth*

Right: **Looking east along the famous sea wall at Dawlish, Devon on a damp 4 November 2005 from the driver's cab.** *John Balmforth*

Above: **Approaching Bristol Temple Meads in a Voyager as another train passes, heading north, on 5 November 2005.** *John Balmforth*

Left: **Driver Team Managers are required to log a specified number of hours at the controls. New Street depot DTM Mark Mosley is seen taking a turn at driving on 13 October 2005.** *John Balmforth*

Below left: **CrossCountry train managers receiving instruction on the coupling rig at Crewe Training Centre on 20 March 2006. This training is necessary because of the continued use of loco-hauled coaching stock on some services.** *John Balmforth*

Customer service

When Charles Belcher took up his post as Managing Director he readily accepted that the company had gone through a trough in which performance - not just of the trains, but customer service too - was below par. Virgin Trains, in striving to be World Class, acknowledges that customer service is at the heart of its operations. To achieve the required level VT aims to exceed customer expectations on a whole range of issues. In September 2000, the company Customer Service Executive Director, Brenda Klug, also fully recognised that Virgin Trains was not world class, but set in place a strategy to deliver that level of service within three years. Indeed, by June 2003 Virgin Trains Passenger's Charter stated:

This is the Passenger's Charter for West Coast Trains Ltd and CrossCountry Trains Ltd, which together operate under the name of 'Virgin Trains'. It sets out our commitment to give you the safe, high quality service you have the right to expect. Any passenger purchasing a ticket for use on services operated by Virgin Trains should enjoy:

▓ a reliable and punctual journey

▓ clean and safe trains and stations

▓ a customer service team member onboard each train to be available to provide help if required

▓ a refreshment service on most trains

▓ a seat if reserved in advance

Copies of this Passenger's Charter will be available at all major stations used by Virgin Trains, from our customer relations team and our website virgin.com/trains.

The Passenger's Charter was intended to be very much passenger-orientated and to achieve its aims consistently would not be easy, especially considering that many trains would literally be running across a building site as the route upgrades progressed. In fact, complaints made by passengers were at an unacceptable level but almost always justified. Many were about performance which was poor with around only 80 per cent of trains managing to run on time, and as

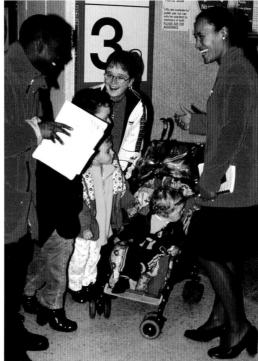

Virgin Trains 'Red Coats' Nicky Walton and Lorna Henry assist a young family on its way at Birmingham New Street on an extremely busy summer Saturday.
Virgin Trains / Milepost 92$^{1/2}$

low as 60 per cent on some Scottish services. This was not surprising considering the ageing locomotives and Mk 3 carriages in use, many of which had been delivered in the 1980s. However, the level of complaints dropped significantly following the introduction of the new train fleets in both Virgin franchises and the near-completion of the upgrade of the southern end of the West Coast Main Line. By 2006, both franchises were

CrossCountry hostess Anna Roccia serves passengers complimentary drinks in a fully occupied first class carriage on an Edinburgh service, on 5 April 2006.
John Balmforth

Above: **CrossCountry Train Manager Karen Beamish carries out revenue protection duties on a very busy Edinburgh service, on 5 April 2006.** *John Balmforth*

Above right: **Karen's brother Peter Dennis, is seen assisting a passenger on Birmingham New Street's crowded platforms.** *John Balmforth*

Right: **CrossCountry Assistant Resources Manager David Heathcock attempts to resolve yet another problem on 23 August 2005.** *John Balmforth*

seeing huge improvements in performance. CrossCountry was achieving the high eighties in percentage terms while at West Coast the figure had reached 90 per cent of trains running on time. This was the level of performance which the Passenger's Charter required for it to have any credibility.

Virgin Trains' own customer research had shown that passengers were essentially looking for the basics (punctuality, cleanliness, information and assistance), but were also looking for the human element whereby staff showed a genuine empathy with customers. Brenda Klug described this as *'service with style.'*

The customer service team recognised that only part of the mission could be achieved from product-driven solutions such as new trains and infrastructure. The rest had to come from the level of personal service that Virgin Trains front line staff could offer. To achieve this, Virgin Trains used the proven theory that if you look after your own people then they will look after the customer. Essentially the front line service could only ever be as good as the staff themselves, including the support processes. This required training,

management, the equipment needed to do the job as well as ensuring that it was there at the right time. Virgin Trains found that it did not matter how good the service was, unless it was provided consistently, it could not be regarded as world class. Again, in Brenda Klug's words: 'Simplistically, the link from satisfied and loyal employees to satisfied and loyal customers to the bottom line is obvious.'

Virgin Trains' customer service team conducted research to identify factors in delivering a world-class service. The study group identified five ingredients which Virgin Trains called the Building Blocks of Great Service:

- customer Focus
- active listening
- teamwork
- empathy
- empowerment.

Turning this into something more tangible to guide recruitment and training evolved Virgin Trains' essential customer service skills:

Virgin Trains' people should:

- be consistent
- treat customers as individuals – not just part of a process
- keep products and pricing understandable
- help customers understand pricing and make the most of the products
- own the problem when things go wrong

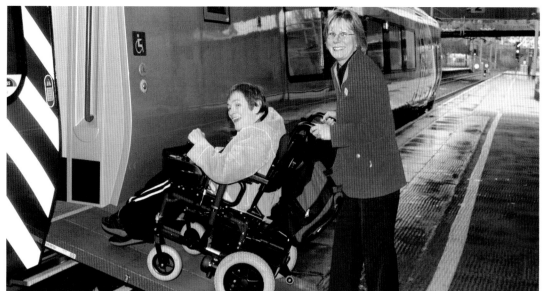

Left: **A Virgin Trains 'Red Coat' helps a wheelchair-bound passenger aboard a Voyager at Coventry in 2003.** *Virgin Trains / Milepost 92¹/²*

Below left: **Virgin Trains' Ron Davies looks up onward travel information for a passenger while colleague Nicola Perkins deals with a telephone enquiry at Birmingham New Street station on 5 April 2006.** *John Balmforth*

Following on from this Virgin Trains introduced:

The Ten Customer Commitments

1. **Look smart in the public eye**
   The way staff look actually says a lot about Virgin Trains

2. **Give Warm Welcomes and Fond Farewells**
   First and last impressions are so important

3. **See each Customer as an individual**
   Everyone wants to be treated as an individual and it helps to make people feel special

4. **Help our Customers wait in comfort**
   The lounges we have created are greatly valued – but not everyone knows about them!

5. **Information belongs to the Customer**
   Our customers buy an arrival time – they must be the first to know of changes

6. **Being there for a Customer**
   Our customers need to feel that they can approach us and ask us anything

7. **Creating the right atmosphere**
   Customers choose the train for a relaxed journey – let's remember that

8. **The Virgin difference**
   Some of our services make us different from other train companies

9. **The bits that get missed**
   It's easy to forget the things which customers rightly take for granted

10. **Doing that little bit extra**
    Go that extra mile – do something special every day for at least one customer or colleague

Among the improvements Virgin Trains increased the number of staff, both at stations and on board trains, and by introducing self-service ticket machines was able to shorten queues at stations. By 2006, Virgin had increased the number of parking spaces at many key stations and attained 'Secure Car Park & Station' status at many locations.

Virgin Trains' Customer Complaints Department was one of the busiest of all the TOCs' during the various upgrade works. Disruptions and problems with both train fleets, saw the department dealing with thousands of complaints every year. Most were about performance and reliability but in general the two companies managed to meet the requirements laid down in their franchise agreements in responding to customer dissatisfaction. However, with the track upgrade, settling in of the new trains and massive improvements in performance, the number of complaints had been more than halved by 2006, and in terms of complaints per passenger Virgin Trains is now one of the best-performing TOCs. With more passengers travelling on West Coast than at any time since 1994 (up by 40 per cent over 2004/05 and continuing to increase), the reduction is a welcome achievement and Virgin Trains satisfaction level is now at its highest since records began in 1999.

Fares

Virgin Trains' main source of income, as with most train operators, comes from government subsidy and fares. The latter hits the passenger's direct 'out-of-pocket' expenditure and because of this fares are a very sensitive and emotive issue. Since the two Virgin Trains companies are carrying almost 94,000 passengers per day between them (June 2006), the potential for discontent is huge. Shortly after privatisation a review of fares carried out by the author revealed 57 different fares between Birmingham and London, although these were spread over three different train companies. Not surprisingly, therefore, passengers often had difficulty in obtaining the best value ticket for the journey being made.

Thankfully the industry has reduced that number but the number of options available is still confusing for some passengers. In Virgin West Coast's case there are now ten different fares between Birmingham and London plus a range of season tickets. In June 2006 the prices of these ranged from £192 for a Virgin Business return in first class to as little as £10 for a Virgin Value Advanced standard class single. Without doubt there are some very attractive bargains available although the competitively priced Value range of tickets does require advance booking and travel is restricted to specific trains. This condition of sale has however, resulted in the cheapest form of travel being out of reach for many of those 'walk-on' passengers who prefer to pay on the day of travel, or who simply cannot book in advance.

When the Virgin Value range of tickets was first introduced, it was only valid for journeys wholly on Virgin Trains services. Recognising the restrictions this placed upon some passengers requirements, VT entered negotiations with other train operating companies and its Value tickets are now available to and from many destinations not served directly by Virgin Trains provided that part of the journey is made on a Virgin service. This facility was not valid for travel on GNER services in mid-2006 however. An example would be a ticket for a passenger wishing to travel from Birmingham to Inverness. Previously, a through Virgin Value ticket would not have been available because Virgin Trains do not operate into Inverness. Passengers would have required either a higher priced through ticket or a Virgin Value ticket to Edinburgh and then a further ticket from Edinburgh to Inverness on Scotrail's service, although both tickets could be purchased before commencing the journey.

The introduction of the Virgin Value ticket range has at times caused confusion. This is because only a limited number of Value tickets are provided and these specific tickets are not available on all services. Passengers sometimes find that they cannot get a Virgin Value ticket because 'the quota has sold out', but a few days later discover that such tickets had become available again. How can this happen? Well, Virgin Trains' 'quota' of Value tickets available is pretty constant, but there is not a regularly set number of tickets for any particular train. On known busy services it would be unwise to allow the availability of cut price tickets to add to the loadings of those trains. Instead, the Value tickets are usually available on trains with known under-utilised capacity. On a service running from say Penzance to Aberdeen a train may have spare capacity on some sections of route, but be fully booked on others. All routes are divided into sections and during each of these train managers are required to pass through the train carrying out a passenger count. That information is then passed to an information centre where it is correlated and from which can be built up a picture of the actual regular usage of the service. This information is then checked and any additional factors added (such as for instance a football match) which may make the service busier over part of its route. At that point a decision can be made as to the number of Virgin Value tickets to be made available for that train and over which parts of the route. Consequently, even though they are on the same train passengers may be able to get a Virgin Value ticket between Plymouth and Bristol or Dundee and Aberdeen, but not between Birmingham and Leeds which is a heavily used section of the route. Equally, if expected normal usage of a particular service is not anticipated to be as high as usual then the quota can be increased on that train.

In 2006, Tony Collins explained that the average fare paid by Virgin Trains' West Coast customers is 7 per cent lower year on year because of the huge increase in ridership. This reflects the number of ticket sales which relate to the cheaper advance purchase tickets. Whilst this is undoubtedly good news for passengers, many of them believe that peak-hour walk-on fares are still too high. Virgin Trains though, can point to the fact that the peak-hour services are very well patronised and the Virgin philosophy that customers will pay for a high-quality service does hold true. Certainly the quality of service is

improving but the important factor now is to continue to improve in this area in order to keep the hard-won custom as well as meeting the anticipated growth in passenger numbers.

For business travellers time is a vitally important commodity. Following the West Coast Main Line upgrade which now sees Pendolino trains running at 125mph over considerable stretches of track, journey times to Liverpool, Manchester and Scotland are being dramatically reduced. Coupled with much improved performance and reliability, this is now seeing Virgin Trains win increasing numbers of passengers from the airlines. After all, Virgin Trains' services run more or less city centre to city centre with no check-in time required such as that at airports. The facilities on the new trains allow business travellers to work uninterrupted during their journey, a factor which also helps make the new services more attractive. In May 2006, West Coast Managing Director Charles Belcher told the author that the passenger split was now approximately 60/40 per cent in favour of the train, a reversal of the figures of a few months before. Despite this it is interesting to note that Virgin West Coast sees the car as its major competitor, and feels that will remain the case until journey times between Glasgow and London are cut still further.

Virgin Trains has received much criticism over the difference in service provided to passengers travelling First Class on its two franchises. On West Coast the First Class fare includes a full English breakfast or refreshments and drinks during the day, all served at seat. It should be noted though, that the West Coast First Class service is aimed at business travellers and most trains carry at least four First Class coaches, the majority of which are full during the peak hours. CrossCountry services on the other hand are usually four or five-car trains and have a limited number of First Class seats provided in one coach only, the company supplying its First Class passengers with a more basic product, still complementary but in snack form.

Virgin Trains argue that the level of business travel on CrossCountry does not support the same level of service as on the West Coast. Many passengers have been confused and do not understand why they seemed to be treated differently when their tickets, carriage insignia and seat antimacassars all clearly stated that they were travelling first class. However, the difference in the price of a first class ticket on the two franchises is significant, with the much higher West Coast fare funding a superior product. In an attempt to distinguish the two levels CrossCountry replaced the first class sections on its trains with 'club class'. By 2006, following requests from passengers, that decision had been reversed with first class being reinstated although still with a lower level of complimentary refreshments.

Complimentary food being served to a passenger travelling first class on a West Coast service on 22 October 2003.
Virgin Trains / Milepost 92$^{1/2}$

Rail/Air links

The Virgin Trains livery is very attractive on the coaches used for the Rail/Air link services, and it is shown to good effect here as a Virgin Atlantic Airbus A340 jets off to distant shores. Although carrying the Milton Keynes–Luton Airport livery the coach was standing in on the Watford–Heathrow run when photographed in 2005. *Virgin Trains*

Early in the franchises Virgin Trains introduced road coaches carrying Virgin Trains livery, operated by National Express, to travel between Watford Junction station and London Heathrow airport. This is a useful frequent service scheduled to take just 40 minutes and calls at each of Heathrow's four terminals, making it valuable to customers of all airlines using the airport. Through tickets are available from many stations across the UK rail network. Passengers requiring assistance between train and coach are able to use the 'journey care' facility to pre-book their assistance and to obtain advice on travel to and from airports.

In addition to the Heathrow service, Stagecoach operates connecting road services using vehicles in Virgin livery between Milton Keynes Central station and London Luton airport. This service is also very popular with non-rail passengers.

Additionally, there is a Rail Air link connection available between Reading and Heathrow. Whilst not a Virgin Trains' service it is a useful connection for passengers travelling to the airport on CrossCountry trains. Once again, services are fast and frequent with through tickets being available.

Many other airports are accessible from the Virgin Trains' network, some of these being:

- *Birmingham International Airport* – Virgin CrossCountry and West Coast operate frequent services calling at Birmingham International station which is adjacent to the airport.

- *Gatwick Airport* – Virgin CrossCountry operates direct services to the station which is located beside the South Terminal.

- *Manchester Airport* – Both West Coast and CrossCountry operate frequent services to Manchester Piccadilly station, from where passengers can get frequent rail connections direct to the airport.

- *Southampton Airport* – Virgin CrossCountry Services call frequently at the station which is located beside the airport.

- *Bristol Airport* – Virgin CrossCountry operates frequent services to Bristol Temple Meads from where there is a dedicated road coach connection to the airport.

The future

Tony Collins told the author that he saw the challenge going ahead as being 'what do you do to build on success?' Even when the original franchise bids were drawn up in 1995/96 there was a realisation that if Virgin Trains was successful it would need more capacity, and for this reason the new train fleets were designed so that extra carriages could be slotted in if required. He feels that there is an inherent demand for rail travel and both CrossCountry and West Coast must continue to meet the Virgin brand value. Up to 2004, Virgin Trains was actually producing a negative brand value within the Virgin Group, but the next two years saw it move into the positive value range.

Growth has resulted in overcrowding on some services and CrossCountry is now seeing huge growth in its business passenger numbers, particularly in first class. This is partly because 'UK plc' is seeing businesses moving out of the traditional bases in London to cities such as Birmingham, Leeds, Manchester, Preston, Sheffield and York which all have thriving economic communities in their own right. CrossCountry is the only train operator that serves most of the major UK cities, and the growth in business travel on its routes reflects the need for these to remain. The Voyager family of trains generally have only 26 first class seats available at present so it is easy to see the problem the increase in business travel is causing, but as Collins says: 'It is a nice problem to have and one which the new franchise must resolve.' CrossCountry accepts that it needs to lengthen the trains, ideally making them all six-car sets and this would allow both additional first and standard class seating, but realistically it will not be possible until the franchise is re-let.

Another issue seen by Tony Collins is the need to make the means of purchasing tickets easier. He does not look upon this as a problem, but an opportunity. He accepts that one of the biggest advantages rail has over other forms of public transport is the availability of walk-up tickets – but the need to manage the increased demand will require the greater use of modern technology. Growth brings more passengers but they in turn do not want to stand in long queues to buy a ticket. Technology is available for advance purchase tickets, now the challenge is to improve the lot of walk-up customers.

Collins also sees further route upgrades as important, citing the Birmingham–Plymouth services as a good example. He said: 'Brunel built a wide-gauge railway which is very twisty and turning but one that would be ideal to upgrade for tilt operation.' Essentially, it costs around £12,500 to install every balise (a trackside transmitter for TASS and ERTMS), but he feels it would make a very sound business case if 35 minutes could be chopped off the journey time. The marketing potential of the route is significant although additional substantial costs would also be incurred to upgrade the infrastructure for increased track forces from higher speed on curves.

Media reports in May 2006 suggested that Sir Richard Branson would walk away from CrossCountry if the new franchise requires cutbacks in quality and becomes a 'bus operator on rails'. I think he is referring to the expectations customers have of the Virgin brand. If so, then he is right – passengers are now getting a high-quality rail service and would see any reduction in quality as a retrograde step. In an in-depth interview with the author, Sir Richard Branson admitted there are some people within the Virgin Group who would prefer Virgin to concentrate on the West Coast franchise, using it as a flagship for the company and not bid to renew the CrossCountry franchise. However, his own feelings are that the staff at CrossCountry have done a good job and are a part of the Virgin family. As such, Sir Richard told me that whilst there are still improvements to be made; emotionally his feeling is to continue and not to listen to those who just say you've got these wonderful Pendolinos, so why take any risks with CrossCountry.

Subsequently, Virgin Rail Group, along with Arriva, First Great Western and National Express was invited to submit a tender for the new franchise. The Virgin bid was submitted by the newly-formed Virgin Voyager Trains Ltd.

By 2006, Virgin's West Coast franchise had seen an increase in passenger numbers over the previous two years of 25 and 15 per cent respectively. Charles Belcher indicated that the company is looking for a further increase of 10 per cent in 2006; but that initial indications are that the figure will need to be revised upwards, such is the growth in rail travel. He said: 'Growth is becoming a problem, a real economic generation of business'.

Virgin's West Coast economic model is to run 50 per cent more trains which will encourage more people to travel by rail, but they will be running out of space by 2010/11. The company is looking ahead at a number of options and these include making the trains longer. Preliminary discussions with Alstom who built the Pendolinos, has revealed that they have the capacity at their factory near Turin to build additional vehicles in time for 2010/11. A decision will need to made sooner rather than later, probably by 2008. Including a tenth carriage in each train set would be straightforward as it would be a trailer vehicle (non-powered), and stations at which West Coast Trains call can generally accommodate trains of that length.

If West Coast growth continues at the present level, and the planned timetable for December 2008 will see a 20-minute frequency from London to Manchester and the West Midlands, VT will need to consider adding an eleventh vehicle, which would need to be powered and would also increase the number of stations where the use of selective door control would be necessary. Adding a twelfth car though is unlikely because at some key locations such as Liverpool Lime Street a 12-car Pendolino would foul the junctions at the station throats

A further option would be to purchase additional Pendolino trains, but finding paths for them to operate around the existing timetable would be almost impossible. Charles Belcher is known to have an aim for line speeds to be increased to 135mph which he believes may be possible with existing signalling, although because braking points would be critical it would be a necessity to have some sort of repeater signal in the cab. Also, the track would have to be further upgraded. Faster trains could facilitate the running of more trains and may be an answer to the phenomenal growth being achieved, although in itself that may have another positive effect on growth. Either way, it cannot be denied that the new upgraded West Coast is rapidly fulfilling Sir Richard Branson's dream of becoming a world-class railway.

Although both of the Virgin Trains franchises operated under letters of agreement with the Department for Transport (DfT), West Coast's situation was different from its CrossCountry sister, in that there was no clause to re-let the franchise if agreement was not reached. As has been seen in CrossCountry's case, the 'no fault termination' clause was invoked by the Strategic Rail Authority and its franchise will be re-let from November 2007, though with a significantly different route network. West Coast, on the other hand, was successful in reaching agreement with the DfT and its franchise resumed its formal status in December 2006, and included some additional routes which will transfer from the present CrossCountry franchise in November 2007.

Four Voyager units were originally built for use on the West Coast Holyhead services, but these have never been used on that route because four-car trains do not have sufficient capacity. Instead, an annual agreement between the two Virgin franchises allows two five-car Super

Voyager tilting trains to be used while the four-car units are operated instead by CrossCountry. It is known that West Coast's requirement for the Holyhead service will increase and further Super Voyagers may have to be used from the CrossCountry fleet.

The changes proposed in the DfT 'New Cross Country Franchise Consultation Document' of June 2006 suggests that these refer to Reading to Brighton and Manchester to Scotland services which will not be part of the new franchise. Nevertheless, some juggling of units is likely to be necessary since all Voyagers that will be required over the West Coast Main Line will need the ability to tilt. Any surplus units could then be used to strengthen services known to be susceptible to regular crowding.

At the beginning of this book I mentioned that prior to winning the CrossCountry and West Coast franchises in 1997, Virgin Rail Group had been unsuccessful in its attempt to obtain open access services along the East Coast Main Line. Since then Virgin has made two more unsuccessful bids for the East Coast franchise. The earlier one, in 2003, included proposals for a high-speed line cutting the journey time between London and Scotland to around two hours. This would have seen brand-new track built alongside congested parts of the present route but using the existing infrastructure where congestion was not a problem. Many pundits predicted that Virgin Rail Group would be successful with its proposals, but the Strategic Rail Authority ended the bidding without awarding the franchise.

When the East Coast Main Line franchise was eventually re-let in 2004 Virgin Rail Group was again amongst the bidders, although the SRA had stated that the high-speed route was not to be included. Ultimately, the franchise was won by the incumbent train operator, GNER. It is rather ironic that now in 2007 the government is giving serious consideration to the building of a high-speed line from London to the North.

Tony Collins told me that even though the gap between the winning bidder second time around and Virgin's bid was substantial (possibly as high as £300 million), both Virgin/Stagecoach bids had been made in earnest, and should the opportunity arise to tender again, the company says it will give it serious consideration. In December 2006 the Department for Transport announced that the East Coast franchise operated by GNER would be operated under a letter of agreement and the franchise re-let in approximately 2008. True to his word, Tony Collins has stated that Virgin Rail Group will be submitting a tender for the franchise.

In concluding, and despite the difficulties experienced by Virgin Trains during the first five years of its franchises, and ultimately whatever the future holds, it is not unreasonable to describe the Virgin Trains story so far as a 'decade of progress'.

Postscript:
A tribute from Milepost 92¹ᐟ²

I t is hardly an exaggeration to say that over the four formative years of Virgin Trains, Milepost 92$^{1/2}$ was almost a part of the Virgin public relations team. In a period where new liveries appeared almost weekly, the red and silver of Virgin's Pendolino and Voyager fleets have remained constant and sparkling. As photographers and a picture library to the railway industry, Milepost 92$^{1/2}$ has appreciated that bright sparkling livery on many occasions as its presence is guaranteed to lift any picture, even on the dullest days, and we are proud of our pictorial documentation of Virgin Trains.

I had many happy adventures when travelling around the world documenting the 'Last Steam Locomotives of the World' but recall many just as exciting when photographing the development and testing of Pendolino and Voyager trains. I recall being commissioned to photograph the test running of the Class 390 on Test Site A in Cumbria. Having sited cameras just north of the River Lune near Tebay, I received a call on my mobile phone from the onboard test team. They told me the train would not stop at Tebay but would pass through at speed en-route from Carnforth to Penrith via the legendary Shap Bank. I innocently responded: 'Oh, you're taking a run at the bank are you?', only to be told: 'This is not a 'Duchess' – the power of this thing is awesome'. This was but one of many trips made to Shap with its scenic grandeur and colourful railway history. From there, we worked in the Lune Gorge and I produced a classic 600mm picture on the curve at Wreay, south of Carlisle – the tightest curve on the West Coast Main Line – of a Pendolino on full tilt.

Milepost 92$^{1/2}$ had a happy association with Virgin Trains right from their early days and produced four magnificent calendars that have gone on to become collector's pieces. Each was crammed with exciting pictures and the stories behind some of these are just as exciting, such as the time when we were on permanent snow alert for a calendar picture. At six in the evening we received a phone call from our contact in the North to say thick snow was falling. I piled my family into the car, headed north and arrived at our hotel around one in the morning. Later that day I was able to take a powerful picture of a Class 87 hauling its train up to Beattock Summit in a blizzard which appeared in the first calendar. On another occasion I drove to Euston in the middle of the night to photograph the first Pendolino to enter the station.

Another unforgettable occasion was when Virgin asked us to film two Pendolinos, coupled together, climbing Beattock Bank at midnight for the 2005 calendar. Beattock Bank at midnight is devoid of any light and the only way the impossible could be achieved was by stringing together floodlights for over a quarter of a mile along the track. But even this ingenuity was insufficient in that, to see the whole train, the camera had to be situated some distance away. To our horror, we found that intervening trees and bushes obliterated the view of the train, and short of calling out the Forestry Commission, the picture had to be made from an artificial viewpoint necessitating the use of a hydraulic platform. Terrified, I was rocketed some sixty feet into the air in total darkness and am told I shouted I would never do anything like this other than for Virgin. The train stopped at Beattock Summit and having secured the picture, I was invited onboard. As I was pulled up from the ballast I was amazed to be confronted by two Virgin hostesses and a chef who, at one in the morning, offered full breakfast! Only the style and panache of Virgin could pull off a stunt like that, and at that time in the morning on Beattock Bank the food tasted better than ever.

Milepost 92$^{1/2}$ recorded the development of both Pendolino for West Coast and Voyager for CrossCountry right from the start and numerous visits were made to Brugge, where Voyager building was going on apace, and to Bombardier's plant at Wakefield. We recorded the first tilting run of the Super Voyager in Southern France in January 2002 and also the arrival of the first Voyager into the specially constructed Central Rivers depot. When Voyagers began through that forgotten sliver of England that is the Cherwell Valley we were there again. Many wonderful pictures were made which appeared in Virgin's press releases and posters.

We were summoned, with great secrecy, to a shoot at Avonmouth Docks to record the arrival of a very special cargo. It turned out to be the very first Pendolino body shell arriving from Italy, and it was to be transported, under wraps, to Alstom's factory at Washwood Heath in Birmingham. Unfortunately, on the day of arrival, Avonmouth was lashed by a force eight gale and, as soon as the lorry, with its top secret load, emerged from the access doors in the bows of the ship, the gale ripped the shroud from its anchor points and, within seconds, the Pendolino was exposed for all to see. However our Colin

Two Pendolinos coupled together illuminated by lineside floodlights photographed by Milepost 92¹/² for Virgin Trains' 2005 calendar, as they climb Beattock Bank.
Virgin Trains / Milepost 92¹/²

Nash did get one picture seconds before the shroud disintegrated and that was used for the press release.

The twin developments of Voyager and Pendolino were always exciting and led to us covering innumerable naming ceremonies nationwide as the new trains went into service. I was so proud when I was told that Sir Richard Branson had put some of our pictures on his office walls. As the building programme progressed so on-line testing got underway and I spent two remarkable weeks at Old Dalby, Alstom's Midlands test centre, recording the first fledgling runs of the Class 390. It was here that we photographed the last testing of 18-car double Pendolinos following brake modifications in 2005. The testing programme represented the last major work of the test track which has since closed.

Our association with Virgin Trains was a long and happy one, producing for them an unrivalled visual record of a period of great change and great technological advance. That they have moved on and achieved higher and higher levels of performance is to be admired. All of us here at Milepost 92¹/² look back on those exciting years with great affection.

Colin Garratt
Director, Milepost 92¹/²
March 2007

Appendices

Appendix A

Technical specifications of the Class 390 Pendolino fleet

Number of trains built	53 nine-car sets
Number of coaches	477
Number of seats	
in fleet	23,373
per nine-car train	441 (145 first + 296 standard)
Maximum speed	140mph
Weight	471 tonnes (coaches 45/55 tonnes)
Maximum power	
at wire	6.7MW
at rail	5.1MW (Class 87 2,500 kW)
	425kW per motor
Train horsepower	6,836 bhp
Electric traction	six propulsion inverters over six cars
Acceleration	0–60mph in 60 seconds (1,000 yards)
	0–125mph in 200 seconds (4 miles)
Braking	Regenerative, Rheostatic, Disc
Brake force	9%g
Safety systems	AWS, TPWS, TASS
	(compatible ERTMS)
Tilt actuation	Electric actuation; max 8 degree
	(TASS over-ride)
TASS	Alstom Signalling/Transport:
	ERTMS compatible
Train length	207 metres (nine-car train)
Availability	87 per cent (46 sets required daily)
Reliability	50,000 miles per casualty (failure)
Toilets	7 (3 disabled toilets)
Wheelchair spaces	three (one first, two standard)
Bicycle spaces	eight
Leasing company	Angel Trains in association with HSBC

Appendix B

Technical specifications for the Voyager/Super Voyager fleet

Class 220 Voyager

Number of trains built	34 four-car sets
Number of seats	188 (42+58+62+26 club class)
Diesel engines	Cummins QSK1, one engine per
	coach (four per train)
	750hp; 559kW at 1,800rpm
	3,000hp per train
Acceleration	0-60mph in 60 seconds
Traction	Two 235kW motors per coach
	(8 per train Alstom ONIX traction
	drive)
Braking	9%g normal service
	12%g emergency
Weight	210 tonnes (52.5 tonnes per coach)
Toilets	three (all disabled standard)
Bicycle spaces	four
Fuel range	1,300 miles

Class 221 Super Voyager

Number of trains built	44 five-car (four four-car sets for
	planned use on West Coast/North
	Wales services)
Number of seats	250 (42+58+62+62+26 club class)
Diesel engines	Cummins QSK1, one engine per
	coach (five per train)
	750hp; 559kW at 1,800rpm
	3,750 hp for five-car train
Traction	Two 235kW motors per coach
	10 per train Alstom ONIX traction
	drive
Acceleration	0-60mph in 70 seconds
Weight	304 tonnes (60.8 tonnes per coach)
Braking	9%g normal service
	12%g emergency
Toilets	four (all disabled standard)
Tilt actuation	Hydraulic: 6 degrees of tilt
Bicycle spaces	four
Fuel range	1,200 miles

Appendix C

Fleet list, numbers and names

Class 390 Pendolino EMUs

390001	*Virgin Pioneer*
390002	*Virgin Angel*
390003	*Virgin Hero*
390004	*Virgin Scot*
390005	*City of Wolverhampton*
390006	*Virgin Sun*
390007	*Virgin Lady*
390008	*Virgin King*
390009	*Virgin Queen*
390010	*Chris Green*
390011	*City of Lichfield*
390012	*Virgin Star*
390013	*Virgin Spirit*
390014	*City of Manchester*
390015	*Virgin Crusader*
390016	*Virgin Champion*
390017	*Virgin Prince*
390018	*Virgin Princess*
390019	*Virgin Warrior*
390020	*Virgin Cavalier*
390021	*Virgin Dream*
390022	*Virgin Hope*
390023	*Virgin Glory*
390024	*Virgin Venturer*
390025	*Virgin Stagecoach*
390026	*Virgin Enterprise*
390027	*Virgin Buccaneer*
390028	*City of Preston*
390029	*City of Stoke-on-Trent*
390030	*City of Edinburgh*
390031	*City of Liverpool*
390032	*City of Birmingham*
390033	*City of Glasgow*
390034	*City of Carlisle*
390035	*City of Lancaster*
390036	*City of Coventry*
390037	*Virgin Difference*
390038	*City of London*
390039	*Virgin Quest*
390040	*Virgin Pathfinder*
390041	*City of Chester*
390042	*City of Bangor / Dinas Bangor*
390043	*Virgin Explorer*
390044	*Virgin Lionheart*
390045	*Virgin Valiant*
390046	*Virgin Soldiers*
390047	*Virgin Atlantic*, renamed *Heaven's Angels*
390048	*Virgin Harrier*
390049	*Virgin Express*
390050	*Virgin Invader*
390051	*Virgin Ambassador*
390052	*Virgin Knight*
390053	*Virgin Mission Accomplished*

Above and above right: **A comparison of the CrossCountry route network shows how closely it parallels much of the UK's motorway network.** *Virgin Trains*

Class 57/3 Thunderbird locomotives

Number	Original Number	Name
57301	47845	*Scott Tracy*
57302	47827	*Virgil Tracy*
57303	47705	*Alan Tracy*
57304	47807	*Gordon Tracy*
57305	47822	*John Tracy*
57306	47814	*Jeff Tracy*
57307	47225	*Lady Penelope*
57308	47846	*Tin Tin*
57309	47806	*Brains*
57310	47831	*Kyrano*
57311	47817	*Parker*
57312	47330	*The Hood*
57313	47371	*Tracy Island*
57314	47772	*Firefly*
57315	47234	*The Mole*
57316	47290	*FAB 1*

Class 220 Voyager DMUs

220001	*Maiden Voyager*, renamed *Somerset Voyager*
220002	*Forth Voyager*
220003	*Solent Voyager*
220004	*Cumbrian Voyager*
220005	*Guildford Voyager*
220006	*Clyde Voyager*
220007	*Thames Voyager*
220008	*Draig Cymraig / Welsh Dragon*
220009	*Gatwick Voyager*
220010	*Ribble Voyager*
220011	*Tyne Voyager*
220012	*Lanarkshire Voyager*
220013	*Gwibir De Cymru / South Wales Voyager*
220014	*South Yorkshire Voyager*
220015	*Solway Voyager*
220016	*Midland Voyager*
220017	*Bombardier Voyager*
220018	*Dorset Voyager*
220019	*Mersey Voyager*
220020	*Wessex Voyager*
220021	*Staffordshire Voyager*
220022	*Brighton Voyager*
220023	*Mancunian Voyager*
220024	*Sheffield Voyager*
220025	*Severn Voyager*
220026	*Stagecoach Voyager*
220027	*Avon Voyager*
220028	*Black Country Voyager*
220029	*Vyajer Kernewek / Cornish Voyager*
220030	*Devon Voyager*
220031	*Tay Voyager*
220032	*Grampian Voyager*
220033	*Fife Voyager*
220034	*Yorkshire Voyager*

Class 221 Super Voyager DMUs

221101	*Louis Bleriot*
221102	*John Cabot*
221103	*Christopher Columbus*
221104	*Sir John Franklin*
221105	*William Baffin*
221106	*William Barents*
221107	*Sir Martin Frobisher*
221108	*Sir Ernest Shackleton*
221109	*Marco Polo*
221110	*James Cook*
221111	*Roald Amundsen*
221112	*Ferdinand Magellan*
221113	*Sir Walter Raleigh*
221114	*Sir Francis Drake*
221115	*Sir Francis Chichester*
221116	*David Livingstone*
221117	*Sir Henry Morton Stanley*
221118	*Mungo Park*
221119	*Amelia Earhart*
221120	*Amy Johnson*
221121	*Charles Darwin*
221122	*Dr Who*
221123	*Henry Hudson*
221124	*Charles Lindbergh*
221125	*Henry The Navigator*
221126	*Captain Robert Scott*
221127	*Wright Brothers*
221128	*Captain John Smith*
221129	*George Vancouver*
221130	*Michael Palin*
221131	*Edgar Evans*
221132	*William Spears Bruce*
221133	*Alexander Selkirk*
221134	*Mary Kingsley*
221135	*Donald Campbell*
221136	*Yuri Gagarin*
221137	*Mayflower Pilgrims*
221138	*Thor Heyerdahl*
221139	*Leif Eriksson*
221140	*Vasco da Gama*
221141	*Amerigo Vespucci*
221142	*Matthew Flinders*
221143	*Auguste Picard*
221144	*Prince Madoc*

Appendix D

Some key facts about Virgin Trains 2004-05

Turnover: £579 million

Government support: £526 million

Track access charges: £441 million

Vehicle leasing costs: £295 million

Drivers: 1,097

Onboard staff: 1,804

Staff at stations: 863

Other staff: 984

Trains operated daily: 398

Train miles per annum: 31.6 million (including empty stock movements)

Passengers carried daily: 93,940

Passengers per annum: 34.1 million

Stations served: 113

Stations operated directly (SFO): 17

New trains: 131 (829 coaches)

West Coast Pendolinos: 53 (477 coaches)

Cross Country Voyagers/Super Voyagers: 78 (352 coaches)

Parliamentary constituencies served: 428

Appendix E

Record-breaking high-speed run, 22 September 2006

Virgin Trains West Coast Main Line record-breaking run from Glasgow Central to London Euston by No 390047 *Heaven's Angels* on 22 September 2006 timing schedule (rounded to the nearest half minute):

Miles	Location	Schedule time	Schedule min.sec	Actual min.sec	mph
0.00	GLASGOW CENTRAL	12:37	0.00	0.00	0
0.66	Eglinton Street Jn	12:39$^{1/2}$	2:30	1.49	33/78
3.83	Rutherglen East Jn	12:43	6.00	4.55	76/75
6.45	Newton	12:45	8.00	6.52	88
8.32	Uddingston Junction	12:46$^{1/2}$	9.30	8.06	92
12.79	MOTHERWELL	12:49$^{1/2}$	12:30	11.03	80
18.26	Law Junction	12:53$^{1/2}$	16.30	15.13	52
26.12	Lanark Junction	12:58$^{1/2}$	21.30	20.21	101
28.60	CARSTAIRS	13:00	23.00	21.56	91
44.38	Abington	13:08$^{1/2}$	31.30	30.17	90
52.50	Beattock Summit	13:14	37.00	35.34	90/128
62.52	Beattock	13:19$^{1/2}$	42.30	41.25	99
76.45	LOCKERBIE	13:26$^{1/2}$	49.30	48.09	124
89.27	Kirkpatrick	13:33	56.00	54.28	127
93.56	Gretna Junction	13:36	59.00	56.48	100
102.28	CARLISLE	13:42	65.00	62.59	23
120.13	PENRITH	13:54	77.00	74.23	110/122
139.18	Tebay	14:06	89.00	86.13	105
152.29	OXENHOLME	14:14$^{1/2}$	97.30	94.38	92
165.14	Carnforth North Jn	14:21$^{1/2}$	104.30	101.42	109/127
169.48	Morecombe Sth Jn	14:23$^{1/2}$	106.30	103.54	110/74
171.40	LANCASTER	14:24$^{1/2}$	107.30	105.12	76
192.38	PRESTON	14:37$^{1/2}$	120.30	119.02	44
197.94	Euxton Junction	14:41$^{1/2}$	124.30	122.40	tsr111
199.92	Balshaw Lane Jn	14:42$^{1/2}$	125.30	123.42	122/126/sig37
207.51	WIGAN N W	14:47	130.00	128.50	81
208.86	Springs Branch Jn	14:48	131.00	129.44	99
213.44	Golborne Junction			132.20	91/100/80
215.83	Winwick Junction	14:52$^{1/2}$	135.30	133.56	81/93

Miles	Location	Schedule time	Schedule min.sec	Actual min.sec	mph
219.24	WARRINGTON BQ	14:54$^{1/2}$	137.30	136.18	91
221.21	Acton Grange Jn	14:55$^{1/2}$	138.30	137.30	102/122
225.28	Preston Brook TNP			139.42	110
226.86	Weaver Junction	14:58$^{1/2}$	141.30	140.34	110/112
234.54	Winsford Signal Box	15:02$^{1/2}$	145.30	144.40	127/128
242.62	Crewe Coal Yard	15:07$^{1/2}$	150.30	148.36	89/78
243.31	CREWE	15:08	151.00	149.11	80/126
248.21	Betley Road			152.04	122/126
251.85	Madeley Junction	15:12$^{1/2}$	155.30	153.49	125/128
262.52	Norton Bridge	15:18	161.00	159.06	90
267.83	STAFFORD	15:21	164.00	162.07	104/77
274.26	Colwich Junction	15:25$^{1/2}$	168.30	166.31	85/tsr82
279.98	Armitage	15:28$^{1/2}$	171.30	169.45	118/123
285.12	LICHFIELD TV	15:31	174.00	172.21	109/125
291.37	TAMWORTH	15:34$^{1/2}$	177.30	175.37	105/126
304.32	NUNEATON	15:41	184.00	182.34	100/128
313.37	Brinklow			187.10	128
318.87	RUGBY	15:50	193.00	190.28	75
321.07	Hilmorton Junction	15:51$^{1/2}$	194.30	192.06	95/114
331.58	Weedon	15:58	201.00	197.28	120/tsr110
344.64	Hanslope Junction	16:04$^{1/2}$	207.30	203.50	127/tsr111
351.57	MILTON KEYNES C	16:07$^{1/2}$	210.30	207.13	127
354.74	Bletchley	16:09$^{1/2}$	212.30	208.55	tsr96/94
364.14	Ledburn Junction	16:14	217.00	213.53	125/128
369.69	Tring	16:16$^{1/2}$	219.30	216.30	125/128
375.08	Bourne End Junction	16:19$^{1/2}$	222.30	219.03	128
383.97	WATFORD Jn	16:23$^{1/2}$	226.30	223.27	112/128
390.01	Harrow & Wealdstone	16:26$^{1/2}$	229.30	226.29	125/126/109
393.39	Wembley Central	16:28$^{1/2}$	231.30	228.08	115/124
396.14	Willesden West L Jn	16:30	233.00	229.39	91
399.76	Camden Junction	16:33	236.00	232.59	55
401.30	LONDON EUSTON	16:36	239.00	235.27	0

tsr = temporary speed restriction
sig = signal check

Note: Unlike on previous speed-record attempts, speed derogations to exceed the permitted line speed could not be given because the Tilt Authorisation Speed Control System (TASS) would have intervened. Without TASS being operative the Pendolino would not have been able to tilt and the record would not have been achieved.

A Virgin Voyager waits for the semaphore signals to clear at Grosmont station during a visit to the North Yorkshire Moors Railway. *railphotolibrary.com*

Acknowledgements

The information contained within this book is to the best of the author's knowledge correct but any inaccuracies notified to him will be amended in any subsequent editions.

The author gratefully acknowledges the assistance provided by the following individuals, organisations and publications without which it would not have been possible to produce this book:

Virgin Trains and the Railway Children Charity for their kind permission to use their logos
Stuart Baker
Shirley Balmforth
Sir Richard Branson
Donald Burgess
Tony Francis
Colin Garratt
Chris Green
Geoff Harris
Michael Hughes
Dennis Lovett
Milepost 92$^{1/2}$
www.railphotolibrary.com
Colin Nash
Eric V. Needham
Peter W. Robinson
Jane Simpson – The Railway Children Charity
John Sears
Will Whitehorn

From Virgin Trains:

Charles Belcher –	Managing Director West Coast Trains Ltd
Nick Chadwick –	West Coast Trains Driver Team Manager, Wolverhampton
Tony Collins –	Chief Executive
Chris Gibb –	Managing Director CrossCountry Trains Ltd
Brian Johnson –	Franchise Director CrossCountry Trains Ltd
Steven Knight –	Corporate Affairs
Arthur Leathley –	Director Corporate Affairs
Mark Mosley –	CrossCountry Driver Team Manager, Birmingham New Street
Kevin Pearce –	Franchise Director West Coast Trains Ltd
Pete Roberts –	Crewe Training Centre
Jim Rowe –	Head of Media Communications

Virgin Trains Driver Training Centre, Crewe
Virgin Trains Media Room
www.virgintrainsmediaroom.com

Voyager No 220018 makes the first through run for 30 years from Wareham to Swanage on 8 September 2002, where it was named *Dorset Voyager* by Moyra Cross and Stan Symes of the Swanage Railway.
railphotolibrary.com

Bibliography

An introduction to the history of the West Coast Main Line, Virgin Trains Media Room (2004)

Capacity Utilisation Policy – Network Utilisation Strategy, Strategic Rail Authority (June 2003)

CrossCountry, Virgin Trains Media Room (2004)

Cross Country: Cinderella to Princess, Virgin Trains Corporate Affairs (2002)

Cross Country Fact File, Virgin Trains (2005)

Cross Country Fact File, British Rail InterCity CrossCountry (1994)

Fact File, Virgin Trains Driver Training Centre, Crewe (2005)

Fares to/from London Euston, CrossCountry Trains and West Coast Trains Ltd (2006)

Full Tilt for West Coast, by Chris Green, Virgin Trains Corporate Affairs (2003)

Losing My Virginity, by Richard Branson, Virgin Books (2004)

Modern Railways, May 2000 page 69, Ian Allan Publishing (2000)

New Dawn – Cross Country: Dream to Reality, Virgin Trains Corporate Affairs (2001)

Passengers Charter, CrossCountry Trains Ltd & West Coast Trains Ltd (2003)

Red Revolution, Virgin Trains Corporate Affairs (2001)

Service with Style, by Brenda Klug, Virgin Trains Corporate Affairs (2000)

Simulation – Features and rail industry application, Virgin Trains Driver Training Centre, Crewe (2005)

The Comprehensive Guide to Britain's Railways 3rd Edition, EMAP Publications (2000)

The Comprehensive Guide to Britain's Railways 7th Edition, EMAP Publications (2004)

The Privatisation of British Rail, Virgin Trains Media Room (2004)

The Virgin Voyager Experience, Rail Passengers Committee North Western England (2004)

Twenty-Five Years of Stagecoach, by Doug Jack, Ian Allan Publishing (2005)

Virgin Trains Airport Connections, CrossCountry Trains Ltd and West Coast Trains Ltd (2003)

West Coast – The Third Dawn, by Chris Green, Virgin Trains Corporate Affairs (2005)

West Coast, Virgin Trains Media Room (2004)

West Coast Main Line – Progress Report May 2006, Department for Transport (2006)

Abbreviations

APT	Advanced Passenger Trains
ATP	Automatic Train Protection
ASLEF	Associated Society of Locomotive Engineers & Firemen
BA	British Airways
CCTV	Closed circuit television
DEMU	Diesel-electric multiple unit
DfT	Department for Transport
DVT	Driving van trailer
DMU	Diesel multiple unit
ECML	East Coast Main Line
ECTS	European Train Control System
EMU	Electric multiple unit
ERTMS	European Railways Train Management System
GNER	Great North Eastern Railway
hp	horse power
HST	High Speed Train
Jn	Junction
kw	kilo-watts
LMS	London Midland & Scottish Railway
MP	Member of Parliament
mpc	miles per casualty
mph	miles per hour
MW	Mega Watts
OPRAF	Office of Passenger Rail Franchising
ORCATS	Operational Research Computer Allocation of Tickets to Services
PIT	Pendolino into Traffic
PTE	Passenger Transport Executive
PTS	Personal Track Safety Certificate
PUG 1	Passenger Upgrade 1
PUG 2	Passenger Upgrade 2
ROSCO	Rolling Stock Company
RPC	Rail Passengers Committee
SFO	Station Facilities Operator
SRA	Strategic Rail Authority
TASS	Tilt Authorisation & Speed Control
TOC	Train Operating Company
UK	United Kingdom
VIP	Very important person
VT	Virgin Trains
WCML	West Coast Main Line
WCRM	West Coast Route Modernisation
WCR 250	West Coast Rail 250

Virgin Trains Network

Regular Services

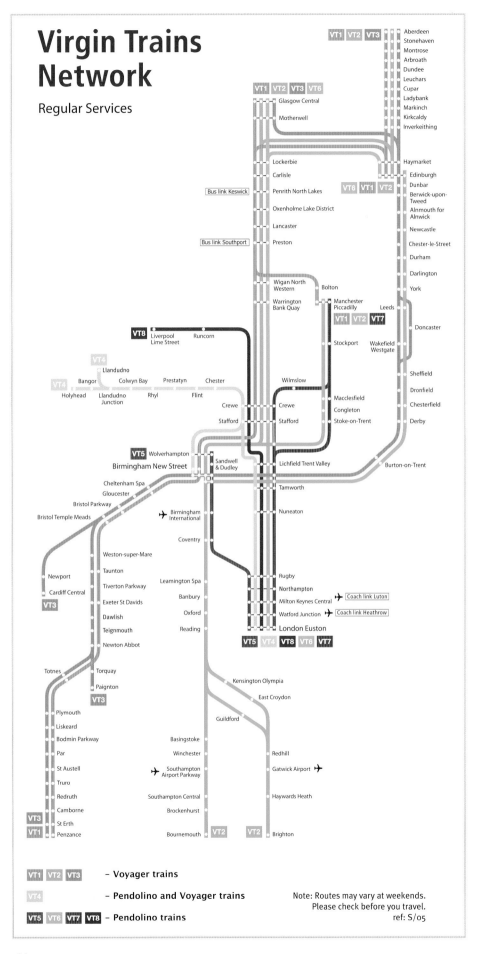

VT1 VT2 VT3	– Voyager trains
VT4	– Pendolino and Voyager trains
VT5 VT6 VT7 VT8	– Pendolino trains

Note: Routes may vary at weekends.
Please check before you travel.
ref: S/05